NEW HAVEN
FROM PURITANISM TO THE AGE OF TERRORISM

New Haveners celebrate the conclusion of World War I on the Green with American flags. One man holds a sign with the words, "WE GOT THE KAISER AT LAST." (Manuscripts and Archives, Yale University Library.)

New Haven

From Puritanism to the Age of Terrorism

Michael Sletcher

ARCADIA

To Teresa and Family

Copyright © 2004 by Michael Sletcher
ISBN 0-7385-2467-0

Published by Arcadia Publishing,
Charleston SC, Chicago IL, Portsmouth NH, San Francisco CA

Printed in Great Britain.

Library of Congress Catalog Card Number: 2004107922

For all general information contact Arcadia Publishing at:
Telephone 843-853-2070
Fax 843-853-0044
E-Mail sales@arcadiapublishing.com
For customer service and orders:
Toll-Free 1-888-313-2665

Visit us on the Internet at http://www.arcadiapublishing.com

CONTENTS

ACKNOWLEDGMENTS

All historians face the dilemma of exclusion; they write their histories with the idea of inclusion but inevitably exclude someone or something. This is not intentional but as historians weave their narrative through time and space, following arrows or signs to some known or unknown destination, they encounter a series of limitations and must forego a comprehensive understanding of the past. As explorers, they are learning themselves, conjuring up images of the past while acknowledging their limitations. Other historians will have to correct their errors and omissions, for there is still no such thing as a comprehensive history. It is as if we are all looking at a Persian carpet, knowing that the shapes and forms might change or rearrange themselves, though the carpet is the same.

Although it is impossible to include everyone and everything over such a large temporal and spatial frame, I have written New Haven's history with the idea of inclusion and have written what essentially might be described as a political, social, economic, religious, and cultural history of an American city and its interaction with other regions (namely New England), the nation (after the early republic), and foreign countries (namely Britain during the colonial period). In so doing, I have attempted to write a linear and coherent narrative, so that the reader might explore some of the patterns as they appeared to me while writing this history.

I would like to thank a number of individuals for their remarks concerning the manuscript. They include David L. Smith of Selwyn College, Cambridge University; Karen Duval, associate editor of the Benjamin Franklin Papers at Yale University; and Alan Graham, chair of the Fifth District of Hamden and former president of the Whitneyville Civic Association.

Historians—to whom I am particularly indebted and whose works have been essential to the writing of New Haven's history—include the late Rollin G. Osterweis, Louis I. Kuslan, Judith A. Schiff, Thomas J. Farnham, Dorothy Ann Lipson, and Ira M. Leonard. I am also indebted to certain individuals who helped me to complete the manuscript. They include Allison Botelho and Bradley Bullis at the New Haven Free Public Libary, Amy Trout and Peter Thomas Lamothe at the New Haven Colony Historical Society, Pamela C. Jordan at the Yale School of Drama Library, and Frank A. Carrano, M.SG. Ret., A.U.S.

~Michael Sletcher

INTRODUCTION

The history of New Haven has received little attention from American colonial historians, whose main focus has been the Massachusetts Bay and Connecticut colonies as well as an assortment of local New England histories. In some ways this is rather peculiar, especially when we consider what the late Perry Miller of Harvard University once said about New Haven as an independent colony:

> The colony of New Haven is the ideal laboratory in which to study the germ of Puritanism; only there can it be isolated and put under the microscope. . . . New Haven was the essence of Puritanism, distilled and undefiled, the Bible Commonwealth and nothing else. . . . Massachusetts contained too many other elements besides Puritanism; it was too large and too complex to achieve in practice an absolute and rigorous working out of the *a priori* philosophy of Puritanism; Connecticut grew up in too haphazard a fashion; Plymouth was too plebeian, in addition to being Separatist, to be completely uncontaminated.

New Haven's uniqueness to other New England settlements was evident from the beginning. The colony adopted John Cotton's "Moses His Judicialls," a law code based on Scripture, which even the Massachusetts Bay Colony did not adopt as a Bible Commonwealth. Consequently, New Haven challenged the British common law tradition and had no trials by jury until its absorption into the Colony of Connecticut in 1665. The colony, moreover, having no official charter, had no organized connection to British chartered companies or commercial associations. Further, its expansion in the early years was not an outgrowth of the main settlement, like other New England settlements and what some historians have termed "sequential town formation." Rather, expansion was as a result of the colonization of more remote places in Connecticut, New York, and New Jersey, where satellite settlements evolved as semi-autonomous colonies under the New Haven Jurisdiction.

This early development underscores the importance of economics as a major driving force behind the early settlements of southern Connecticut, for although religion defined the puritan mind and its migration to the New World, the coastline offered economic opportunity for transatlantic trade and commercial enterprises. Indeed, of the first generation, the overwhelming majority—including Theophilus Eaton, Thomas Gregson, and Stephen

Goodyear—were London merchants and envisaged their migration as not only an opportunity to establish a godly kingdom on Earth, but as a venture to establish a commercial center along the eastern seaboard, competing with the Dutch in New Amsterdam, the French in Quebec, and even with fellow English Puritans to the north. Consequently, when about 500 Puritans left Boston to settle another region, it was only natural that they chose a site along Long Island Sound, where they had received favorable reports of a natural harbor and its surrounding land. And having brought with them £36,000 in capital—by far the largest investment of all the New England settlements—they attempted to set up a commercial center, establishing a direct trade route with England. Nevertheless, this project failed either through misfortune or poor judgment.

In an age when economics, politics, and religion were so intertwined that any thought of separating them was unimaginable to the historical agents, commercial pursuits and political maneuvering were deferential to the religious idealism of the Puritan founders and their progeny. Even the founding of Yale College in 1701 had religious significance for the training of a ministry. With the breakdown of religious orthodoxy in the eighteenth and nineteenth centuries, the Yankee character emerged with its rugged simplicity and capitalist ingenuity, but religion remained an important component of New Haven and the region as a whole. Even to this day it would be a mistake to underestimate its influence, or as Jon Butler has pointed out in *Awash in a Sea of Faith* (1990):

> Despite complaints of "secular humanism" and eroding religious values, over 97 percent of Americans polled on religion expressed a belief in God, and 60 percent regularly attended public worship, figures that stood in marked contrast to polls in Western Europe, where 40 percent of respondents said they did not believe in God and less than 10 percent regularly attended church.

The breakdown of religious orthodoxy simply meant that different forms of religion and different sects emerged in New Haven, like Anglicanism, Baptism, and Unitarianism, and as larger numbers of immigrants came to the city, Catholicism and Judaism.

The arrival of European immigrants during the nineteenth century provided a new cultural identity for the city as Irish, Germans, Italians, and eastern Europeans—mostly Russian Jews—arrived *en masse*. New Haven's growing prosperity during the early republic had made it a wealthy hub of commercial activity and later as a manufacturing center of the United States. Its industrial growth made it more attractive to immigrants fleeing political and economic hardships in nineteenth- and twentieth-century Europe. At the same time, industrialists took advantage of this new source of cheap labor. Other immigrant groups, especially after the anti-immigrant laws of the 1920s, arrived in the city. African Americans, who had been brought to New Haven as slaves during the colonial period, arrived from the South after the Civil War and in larger numbers after World War I. Puerto Ricans arrived after World War II, but today New Haven is a conglomeration of ethnic identities, comprising a multitude of countries and generations of mixed marriages.

Recently New Haven's growth and prosperity has come into question as an economic downturn in the second half of the twentieth century has resulted in the flight of many, mostly white, middle- and upper-middle-income groups to the suburbs. At the same time, many manufacturers and retailers have gone out of business or left the city, leaving the city with high rates of unemployment while the population exodus has resulted in a smaller tax base. New Haven's economic recovery is still in flux as city officials attempt to find a solution and deal with the added cost of protecting the city against a terrorist act. The task is daunting, but if there is one lesson to learn it is that the history of New Haven is about change and continuity: from economic hardship to prosperity; from peace to war; from slavery to freedom; from immigration to acculturation and diversity; from displacement to assimilation; and from decay to renewal.

ABBREVIATIONS USED IN TEXT:
NHFPL: New Haven Free Public Library
YUL: Manuscripts and Archives, Yale University Library
NHCHS: New Haven Colony Historical Society

Chapter One

PURITANISM AND THE BREAKDOWN OF RELIGIOUS ORTHODOXY

The early history of New Haven is the story of the original inhabitants, known as Native Americans, American Indians, Indians, or Amerindians. Millennia earlier, their ancestors had crossed the Bering Strait from eastern Siberia to Alaska and Canada, and then migrated eastward and southward. When the European explorers and adventurers arrived in the late fifteenth century, a variety of cultural and linguistic groups had evolved in North, Central, and South America.

During the sixteenth and seventeenth centuries, the Quinnipiack Indians, tributaries to the powerful Mohawk and Pequot tribes to the north and east, lived along the natural harbor of present-day New Haven, where a large river and smaller estuaries flowed into the Sound. A semi-sedentary people speaking the Quiripi dialect of the Algonquian language, and whose name probably meant "long water" or "river place," the Quinnipiacks were neighbors of the Mohegans and Pequots. They hunted wild animals like deer and fowl, harvested shell and scale fish, and collected roots, nuts, and fruits. They farmed the land too, supplementing their diet with corn, beans, and squash. European epidemics reduced their numbers, so when the English came to the region in 1638, they numbered about 150 persons, of whom 46 were fighting men.

The Quinnipiack soon exchanged their lands for a few articles and promises of protection from the Puritans against marauding Indian tribes, namely the Mohawks. They lived on the eastern side of the harbor, on a 30-acre reservation, on what became the first Indian reservation in British North America. Their numbers were small, and by the end of the colonial period the remaining Quinnipiack, numbering a few men and women, moved northward to Farmington where they joined the Tunxis tribe. Native historian John William De Forest has explained their ordeal:

> Knowing little of European modes of life and judging of the colonists greatly by themselves, they supposed that the latter would cultivate but a little land, and support themselves, for the rest, by trading, fishing and hunting. Little did they think that in the course of years the white population would increase from scores to hundreds, and from hundreds to thousands; that the deep forests would be cut down; that the wild animals would disappear; that the fish would grow few in the rivers; and that the poor remnant of the Quinnipiacs would eventually leave the graves of their forefathers, and wander away into another land. Could they have anticipated that

> a change so wonderful, and in their history, so unprecedented, would
> of necessity follow the coming of the white man, they would have
> preferred the wampum tributaries of the Pequots and the scalping
> parties of the Five Nations, to the vicinity of a people so kind, so
> peaceable, yet so destructive.

The Puritan settlers of New Haven were, as De Forest has concluded, "perhaps, not less worthy of praise than the quakers of Philadelphia for the peace and quietness which invariably existed between them and the aborigines." Relations between the two parties were generally good throughout the colonial period, but the Quinnipiack were also a friendly people whose numbers were small and who posed no real threat to the Puritan establishment.

The first settlers had sailed from England to the Massachusetts Bay Colony under the leadership of Theophilus Eaton, a wealthy London merchant, and John Davenport, the late pastor of St. Stephen's Church on Coleman Street in London. Although most of them had come from Davenport's London parish, others had come from Kent and Hertfordshire. After some delay by a government impressment of the ship *Hector*, they left London in late April or early May 1636 and arrived in Boston on June 26. It is not certain whether they had intended to join the Massachusetts Bay Colony or to establish their own settlement, as there is no surviving record of their original agreement, but whatever might have been the case, they soon set their sights on the "rich and goodly meadows" of the Quinnipiac. They had already heard favorable reports of the harbor and land there from Captain Israel Stoughton and Captain John Underhill, who had recently been pursuing the Pequot Indians through that territory. Eaton and Davenport immediately made preparations to investigate the area, and at the end of August, little more than two months after they had landed in Boston, Eaton and a company of men went to investigate the reports, returning with a favorable impression of the land and harbor.

The following April, Davenport and a group of about 500 Puritan followers set sail for the Quinnipiac. They arrived on April 24 and set up camp on Long Island Sound. Having no charter or legal claim to the land, they negotiated a series of treaties with the local Indians, increasing their land possessions over the next decade. The first and most crucial of them was in November 1638 in which Momauguin, the leader of the Quinnipiac, offered the settlers the lands around the harbor in exchange for "twelve coats of English trucking cloth, twelve alcumy spoons, twelve hatchets, twelve hoes, two dozens of knives, twelve porringers, and four cases of French knives and scissors," as well as "a portion of ground on the East Side of the Harbour" and promises of protection against the Mohawks, who had been making raids against the Quinnipiac and other tribes in the area. The second treaty was in December 1638 in which the sachem Montowese, living beyond East Rock, granted the settlers lands on both sides of the Quinnipiac River in exchange for "eleven coats made of trucking cloth, one coat for [Montowese] of English cloth, made up after the English manner, [and] a piece of land by the river for [the sachem's] men," who numbered no more than ten warriors at the time of the agreement. In May of 1645, a third and final treaty was signed, confirming the settlers' land holdings, which included the lands of present-day New Haven, Hamden, North Haven, East Haven, Branford, North Branford, Wallingford, Cheshire, and sections of Woodbridge, Orange, Bethany, Prospect, and Meriden.

In some ways the settlement of the Quinnipiac was similar to the English village, but the wilderness forced the settlers to adapt themselves to the foreign environment. For defensive reasons, the town was built around nine square grids, of which eight surrounded the central one called the "market place." There were two additional suburban sections extending to the waterfront (then much closer to the central part of New Haven than it is today). On these grids the settlers built their houses, of which John Brockett's map of 1641 tells us the names and home lots of the first generation. According to Brockett's map, the original investors of plantation received fair-sized lots around the market place, whereas those who had not been the original investors (at least 32 families) were given lots outside the 11-division perimeter (see illustration on page 65).

Among the first settlers were a large number of wealthy merchants. Unlike other settlements in New England, commerce was a central feature of the colony's beginnings. This was largely due to the parishioners of St. Stephen's, who had come from a non-conformist and merchant stronghold of London, and who set their sights on building a commercial hub on the eastern shore of the New World. The natural harbor and water connections of the Quinnipiac undoubtedly contributed to the location of the settlement, but there was also an interest in agriculture, as the early reports of fertile land suggest. These reports, however, proved to be overly optimistic. The land was at best moderately fertile and varied greatly from one region to the next. Consequently, the colony during the seventeenth and eighteenth centuries did not prosper in agriculture and stock raising, as the original settlers had intended. Nor did it profit from the lucrative fur trade since competing interests in the region—including the French, Dutch, Swedish, and other English settlements—already dominated the market.

On June 4, 1639, the 70 proprietors met in Robert Newman's barn "to compare views and settle upon a plan of civil government according to the word of God." After some deliberation, they agreed to give only church members the vote and right to hold office. This was similar to the Massachusetts and Plymouth models, but New Haven would soon go further by adopting John Cotton's "Moses His Judicialls," a code of laws based on the Scriptures. The proprietors then proceeded to select 12 (later reduced to 11) men to choose seven of their number to create a church. The Seven Pillars, as they were known, included Davenport, who was selected to be pastor of the First Church, a position he held until leaving the colony in 1668. On August 22, the church began its services, first outdoors or in Newman's barn and later in the 50-foot-square meetinghouse built on the marketplace in 1640. The Seven Pillars met again on October 25 and formed themselves into a General Court. They added nine more men to their number and proceeded to select a magistrate and four deputies. These were annual offices—comprising the executive, legislative, and judicial—and Eaton was chosen as the first magistrate, a position he held until his death in 1658.

On September 1, 1640, the General Court renamed the settlement "Newhaven" and by the following year the population had grown to about 800 settlers. The colony also expanded to include a series of detached settlements, which fell under the New Haven Jurisdiction. The Reverend Peter Prudden, with settlers from Hertfordshire, founded Milford in 1639, and Reverend Henry Whitefield founded Guilford that same year (see illustration on page 66). In 1641, Reverend Richard Denton, with a breakaway group from the Wethersfield settlement, founded Stamford while a group of settlers founded Southold on the eastern end of Long Island. In 1644, the Reverend Abraham Pierson founded Branford. Other settlements came under the New Haven Jurisdiction. Greenwich, which was an extension of Stamford, was founded in 1640, and that same year a group of prominent New Haven settlers formed the Delaware Company, sending about 50 families as far south as present-day Salem, New Jersey, and to Philadelphia to profit from the fur trade. The company and adventure failed in the end, largely as a result of competing Dutch and Swedish interests in the area, as well as a devastating epidemic. However, New Haveners continued to assert their claims on the region until the Duke of York took title of the lands between the Delaware and Connecticut Rivers, and the New Haven Jurisdiction fell apart, ending with the absorption of each New Haven town into the Colony of Connecticut.

With no royal patent or legal claim to lands in North America, the New Haven colonists, before leaving England, might have come to some sort of understanding with either Hugh Peter or George Fenwick regarding the Warwick grant, but no evidence points in that direction. Even if they had, their claims remained legally suspect. Consequently, they set out to legitimize their enterprise, first by obtaining a copy of the Massachusetts Charter and claiming their right to settle on the Delaware River. This having failed, they decided to obtain their own royal charter. They appointed Thomas Gregson, a wealthy merchant, to go to England and negotiate a patent for the colony, advising him to join with Connecticut and obtain a joint patent for the two colonies. Gregson, however, was lost at sea and Connecticut acted alone in 1645, asking Fenwick to enlarge the Warwick grant and provide Connecticut with a patent of its own. In the end, neither colony received a patent and New Haven was still without a charter.

In the winter of 1646, Gregson left for England on board the ship New Haveners have since called the "*Phantom Ship*." In an attempt to open a direct trade route with England, a group of merchants at New Haven contracted John Wakeman, Joshua Atwater, Jasper Crane, and Richard Miles to build an oceangoing vessel. With a cargo of wheat, peas, hides, beaver, and peltry valued at over £5,000, the ship set sail for England in the middle of January and was never heard from again. Among the passengers of the ill-fated voyage were prominent men and women including Captain George Lamberton, Captain Nathaniel Turner, Francis Austin, and the wife of Stephen Goodyear. As told by Cotton Mather in the *Magnalia Christi*, the godly people of New Haven, having heard nothing about their ship for some time, prayed for a sign and, in the summer of 1647 after a great thunderstorm, an apparition appeared in the form of a ship sailing northward through the mouth of the harbor. Her "sails filled under a fresh gale, holding her course north, and continuing under observation, sailing against the wind for the space of half an hour," the spectators of New Haven watched her sail towards them and then dissipate into thin air. Davenport, reading the vision as a providential message from God, declared that their prayers for a sign had been answered and the legend has persisted ever since *(see illustration on page 66)*. In 1850, poet Henry Wadsworth Longfellow retold the story in verse, romanticizing the legend:

> In Mather's Magnalia Christi,
> Of the old colonial time
> May be found in prose the legend
> That is here set down in rhyme.
>
> A ship sailed from New Haven
> And the keen and frosty airs,
> That filled her sails at parting
> Were heavy with good men's prayers.
>
> "O Lord! If it be they pleasure"
> Thus prayed the old divine—
> "To bury our friends in the ocean,
> Take them, for they are thine!"
>
> But Master Lamberton muttered,
> And under his breath said he,
> 'This ship is so crank and walty
> I fear our grave she will be!'
>
> And the ships that came from England
> When the winter months were gone
> Brought no tidings of the vessel
> Nor of Master Lamberton.
> This put the people to praying
> That our Lord would let them hear

What in his great wisdom
He had done with friends so dear.

And at last their prayers were answered:—
It was in the month of June,
An hour before sunset
Of a windy afternoon.

When steadily steering landward,
A ship was seen below,
And they knew it was Lamberton, Master,
Who sailed so long ago.

Oh she came with a cloud of canvas
Right against the wind that blew
Until the eye could distinguish
The faces of the crew.

Then fell her straining topmasts,
Hanging tangled on the shrouds;
And her sails were loosened and lifted
And blown away like clouds.

And the masts with all their rigging,
Fell slowly one by one,
And the hulk dilated and vanished,
As a sea-mist in the Sun!

And the people who saw this marvel
Each said unto his friend,
This was the mould of their vessel
And thus her tragic end.

And the pastor of the village
Gave thanks to God in prayer
That to quiet their troubled spirits
He had sent this Ship of Air.

New Haven's failure to form a direct trade route with England, together with the failure of the Delaware Company, had a devastating effect on the colony. Instead of becoming a commercial center with extended tributary towns, it turned into a small agricultural settlement by the second half of the seventeenth century and was commercially dependent on Boston and New Amsterdam. Also contributing to this economic downturn were the English civil wars. From 1639 to 1641, New Haven had experienced a demographic boom, its population increasing from about 500 to about 800 settlers, but by the beginning of the civil wars (1642), immigration had come to a standstill and a pattern of reverse migration was taking place. Prominent citizens like Samuel Eaton, Thomas James, and William Hooke returned to England where they joined in the parliamentarian struggle against the king.

Puritanism and the Breakdown of Religious Orthodoxy

Although many settlers returned to the mother country, others like John Davenport and Theophilus Eaton stayed behind and fought the parliamentarian struggle by writing pamphlets and holding public days of fast and prayer. Of all the New England settlements, no other supported the parliamentarian cause more than New Haven. In 1643, the General Court established days of fast and prayer for the parliamentarian forces, and that same year the oath of allegiance to be taken by all magistrates excluded any mention of the king. The Court also saw the opportunity to procure a charter for New Haven, "judging it a fit season now for that end," but alas they put their agent aboard the phantom ship and never heard from him again.

Their loyalty to the parliamentarian cause, however, was rewarded in 1648 when a joint committee of the two Houses of Parliament recognized New Haven as a colony. Their influence continued into the commonwealth period when Henry Whitefield and other prominent settlers wrote to Oliver Cromwell about their suspicions of an impending Dutch attack. Cromwell responded by sending four ships and a contingent of troops to capture New Amsterdam, but by the time the fleet arrived in North America, the first Anglo-Dutch War (1652–1654) had concluded and the mission was aborted. With the restoration of Charles II on May 12, 1660, the colony remained obstinate and was the last of all the New England settlements to recognize the new king, delaying its official recognition of the Stuart monarchy until August 22, 1661, almost a year and a half after Charles landed at Dover. The General Court declared the following:

> Although we have not received any forme of proclamation by order from his Majestie or Counsell of State for the proclaiming his Majestie in this Colony, yet the Court taking incouragement from what hath bene in the rest of the United Colonies, hath thought fit to declare publiquely and proclaime, that we do acknowledge his Royal Highness, Charles the Second, King of England, Scotland, France and Ireland, to be our Soveraigne Lord and King, and that we do acknowledge ourselves the inhabitants of this Colony to be his Majesties loyal and faithful subjects. GOD SAVE THE KING.

Having delayed the recognition of the monarchy, New Haven did something more daring: It sheltered three of the 59 regicides who had signed the death warrant of Charles I in 1649: Edward Whalley, William Goffe, and John Dixwell, whose names had appeared on the royal proclamation of June 6, 1660, "being deeply guilty of that most detestable and bloody treason, in sitting upon, and giving judgment against the life of our Royal Father." At the end of the proclamation was the following warning from His Majesty: "And that no person or persons shall presume to harbour or conceal any the persons aforesaid, under pain of misprision of high treason." These words, though clearly a declaration of severe consequences, were to have little effect on the Puritans of New England.

New Haven

The story of the three regicides in New England begins with Generals Goffe and Whalley leaving Gravesend, London, two days after Charles had been proclaimed king, and sailing to New England under the aliases Edward Richardson and William Stephenson. Arriving at Boston on July 27, they lived at the Cambridge house of Major Daniel Gookin for the next seven months and assumed their natural identities, going about their business as if no restoration had taken place. It was not long before Captain Breedon, a royalist, carried news back to England of their whereabouts. Sensing the displeasure of the king, Governor John Endicott and his council debated the issue of what to do next.

While debating, Goffe and Whalley disappeared into the wilderness and after a brief sojourn at Hartford, where they were greeted warmly, they came to New Haven in early March of 1661. For the next three weeks they were guests at the house of the Reverend Davenport, who is said to have preached a sermon to his New Haven congregation in which he exhorted the following from the Book of Isaiah (16:3-4): "Hide the outcasts; don't betray the fugitives; let my outcasts dwell with thee." There can be no doubt that the settlers of New Haven were sympathetic toward the regicides, but when news of an English reward for their arrest reached New Haven, the two men disappeared again, this time in the direction of New Amsterdam, or so they pretended. After reaching Milford, they turned back at night and returned to New Haven, where Davenport and others hid them for the next few months.

The royal order for the arrest of Whalley and Goffe eventually reached Boston and Governor Endicott reluctantly forwarded it to the magistrates of New Haven. The royalists Thomas Kellond and Thomas Kirk were charged with the order and arrived at the Guilford house of Governor William Leete on May 11, where the governor of the New Haven Colony proceeded to read the order aloud with the intention of sending word to Whalley and Goffe that the king's agents were in the vicinity. Kellond and Kirk interrupted Leete, saying that the order should not be read in public and asking the governor for a search warrant and horses so that they might fulfill their commission. The governor stalled for time, delaying the arrival of the horses and informing the agents that he could not provide them with a search warrant until consulting with the other magistrates of the colony, but said that he would write a letter immediately for that purpose. By the time the horses arrived and Leete had written his letter to the other magistrates, it was nightfall and too late to travel. The next day was Sunday and, according to New Haven law, no one could travel on the Sabbath. The agents had to wait until Monday before traveling to New Haven. After they left, Leete followed them at a slow pace and convened the magistrates of the colony. The meeting took so long that the king's officials finally asked the magistrates whether they intended to honor the king's order or not, to which Leete responded, "We honor his Majesty, but we have tender consciences." By the time a search warrant was granted, Kellond and Kirk had become agitated and knew that a search would prove futile. They proceeded toward New Amsterdam and then returned to Boston empty handed.

Having been warned on Saturday that the king's officials were searching for them, Whalley and Goffe had disappeared quickly but had not gone far. For the greater part of the summer they hid in the surrounding wilderness or in a cave on the top of West Rock, now called "Judges' Cave." Richard Sperry, a farmer living close by, and his sons left food on a stump at the foot of West Rock, and on a few stormy nights the judges apparently ventured down the Rock and stayed at Sperry's house. Few New Haveners knew where they were hiding and when the search came to a halt in August, the men fled to Milford where they spent the next three years in relative peace. The threat of a new search brought them back to the cave on West Rock, but they soon decided to leave New Haven after an Indian party discovered the cave while hunting. They traveled northward as far as Hadley, Massachusetts, on the western frontier of the Bay Colony. For the next 12 to 15 years they lived in Hadley, concealed by the Reverend John Russell. Whalley died there and shortly afterwards Goffe left for Hartford where he too might have died, but little is known about him or his whereabouts thereafter.

An earlier story about Goffe reveals that, during King Philip's War (1675–1676), an Indian party attacked Hadley while the residents were observing a fast day at the meetinghouse. They had their arms with them, but confusion ensued and a tall, stout man, dressed in a white robe and carrying a sword, appeared out of nowhere, taking command of the residents and repelling the Indian invasion. As quickly as he had appeared, the unknown man disappeared into the wilderness and the settlers thought that God had sent an angel to protect them until years later when they learned that the deliverer of Hadley was Goffe himself. Such stories have become part of New England legend and while there may be some question about their historical accuracy, one might find pleasure in them, as did Sir Walter Scott and James Fenimore Cooper, both of whom included the Goffe story in their writings: the former in his *Peveril of the Peak* and the latter in his *Wept of Wish-ton-Wish*.

The third regicide, Colonel John Dixwell, arrived in New England after Whalley and Goffe had left New Haven for Hadley. He joined them there before coming to New Haven himself, where he lived on the corner of Grove and College Streets in a house that was indentified as "Old Dixwells" on the map of 1714 and "Joh. Thompson, Formerly Col. Dixwells" on James Wadsworth's map of 1748 *(see illustration on page 67)*. Unlike Whalley and Goffe, the agents did not search for him, for they assumed he had died in Europe. Nonetheless, Dixwell retained his alias James Davids and married Joanna, the widow of Benjamin Ling. After she passed away, he married Bathsheba Howe in Wallingford, with whom he had three children. In a stanza from Ezra Stiles's long poem on the regicides, he:

> felt the force of human ties—
> Him to Quinnipiack led the social flame;
> A borrowed appellation gave disguise;
> He reared a family and rose to fame.

Dixwell apparently did not reveal his true identity until he was on his death bed, but certain New Haveners—like his friend and neighbor the Reverend James Pierpont—knew about his identity and kept it a secret from others. On March 18, 1689, Dixwell died and was laid to rest in the old burying-ground on the marketplace behind what is today Center Church. Of the three regicides, he was the only one to die and be buried in New Haven itself.

Such acts of defiance against the Stuart monarchy must have provoked a reaction from Charles II and some would even say that the absorption of the New Haven Colony into the Connecticut charter was Charles's revenge. Although the story is far more complicated than this, Charles certainly displayed no sympathies for the colony and made his displeasure known before July 1661 when Boston sent word to the New Haven Jurisdiction that the king was annoyed by the colony's failure to apprehend the regicides, especially "when it was publicly known that they were in New Haven." In the letter from the Massachusetts Bay Colony dated July 4, 1661, the governor's secretary expressed the king's displeasure at the colony and added the following:

> Further I am required to signify to you as from them [the Massachusetts Council], that the non-attendance with diligence to execute the king's majesty's warrant for the apprehending of Colonel Whalley and Goffe will much hazard the present state of these colonies and your own particularly, if not some of your persons, which is not a little afflictive to them. And that in their understanding there remains no way to expiate the offence and preserve yourselves from the danger and hazard but by apprehending the said persons, who as we are informed are yet reamaining in the colony and not above a fortnight since were seen there, all which will be against you. Sir, your own welfare, the welfare of your neighbours, bespeak your unwearied pains to free yourself and neighbours.

New Haven received the Massachusetts missive on July 30. The General Court, convening on August 1, responded with declarations of naiveté and innocence:

> And as for that you note of our not so diligent attendance to his majesties warrant, . . . it was not done out of any mind to slight or disown his majesties authority, . . . nor out of favour to the Colonels, nor did it hinder the effect of their apprehending, they being gone before the warrant came into our colony, as it is since fully proved; but only there was a gainsaying of the gentle[men's] earnestness, who retarded their own business to wait upon ours without commission; and also out of scruple of conscience and fear of unfaithfulness to

our people, (who committed all our authority to us under oath,) by owning a general governor [Governor Leete], unto whom the warrant was directed, as such implicitly, and that upon misinformation to his majestie given, though other magistrates were mentioned, yet (as some thought) it was in or under him, which oversight (if so it shall be apprehende[d]) we hope, upon our humble acknowledgement, his majestie will pardon, as also that other and greater bewailed remissness in one, in not securing them till we came and knew their place, out of over-much belief of their pretended reality to resign up themselves, according to their promise to save the country harmless, which failing is so much the more lamented, by how much the more we had used all diligence to press for such a delivery upon some of those that had shewed them former kindness, as had been done other where, when as none of the magistrates could otherwise do any thing in it, they being altogether ignorant where they were or how to come at them, nor truly do they now, nor can we believe that they are hid any where in this colony, since that departure or defeatment.

Interestingly enough, New Haven sent this missive to Boston just three weeks before the colony officially recognized the restoration of the Stuart monarchy, indicating that the leading magistrates were now trying to appease the king for their failure to apprehend the regicides.

Without a charter, New Haven was in a vulnerable position constitutionally, and when the magistrates learned that Connecticut was about to seek royal approval for a charter, Governor Leete began a correspondence with Governor John Winthrop Jr. in the hope that the Connecticut governor would obtain a patent for both colonies. Winthrop, after some months in London, eventually obtained a charter from Charles, but in a premeditated and cunning move on the part of Winthrop and the Connecticut Colony, he obtained a charter recognizing the territory of New Haven as part of the jurisdiction of Connecticut.

New Haven's days as an independent colony were coming to an end and the satellite towns, seeing the shift of power, began to annex themselves to the Connecticut Colony. In June of 1662, almost two months after Charles had issued the charter, Southold left the New Haven Jurisdiction for Connecticut. Stamford and Greenwich followed suit and Guilford prepared to do the same by the end of 1662. Milford, Branford, and New Haven were the last of the New Haven Jurisdiction to hold out, with Milford joining in 1664, and Branford and New Haven holding out until the end when, in 1665, they too were absorbed into Connecticut under the charter of 1662.

New Haveners, namely the conservative faction, were outraged by the Connecticut takeover and held out until the bitter end, but the destiny of the colony had already been determined; they had displeased the king in the early 1660s and were now about to pay the price. On March 12, 1664, Charles II granted the lands between the Delaware and Connecticut Rivers to his brother, the Duke of York, who was planning an invasion of New Amsterdam. Despite the new charter, recognizing the boundaries of Connecticut as far as Long Island Sound, Charles inadvertently gave half of Connecticut away to his brother James until a royal commission agreed that the boundaries extended to the Sound, as stated in the charter of 1662. New Haven was now in a difficult position: either join Connecticut with its charter or become a royal colony under an Anglican (and suspected Catholic) regent. On December 15, it came to the logical conclusion to merge with her sister colony to the north, despite the protestations of some conservatives like John Davenport, who would have agreed with part of the formal submission act of January 5, 1665, claiming that the merger was "from a necessity brought upon us by . . . Connecticut."

The merger had a number of ramifications for the small colony. On the one hand, Connecticut had subscribed to the Half-Way Covenant, a New England compromise by which the children of church members received baptism and partial church membership. New Haven, on the other hand, had adhered to a strict form of Calvinism, and with its absorption into Connecticut it was now expected to adopt the Half-Way Covenant. What is more, the franchise of Connecticut was more open, extending to non-church members 21 years of age or older who held "a 20 pound estate in housing or land." Trial by jury, a common law tradition practiced by all other New England settlements, was introduced for the first time, further eroding the rule of the saintly class. The conservatives were in a vulnerable position, but challenged the merger nonetheless. John Davenport, one of the original founders, was so annoyed by the event that he eventually left New Haven in 1667 and took over the First Church in Boston, where he died shortly afterwards in 1670, and was buried next to his old friend John Cotton. Other conservatives, opposed to the more liberal franchise, founded new settlements outside of Connecticut. The Reverend Abraham Pierson of Branford and Robert Treat of Milford founded Newark, New Jersey, in 1673. Other settlements like Wallingford (1670) and Derby (1675) were also a reaction to the merger.

A new threat to New Haven's orthodoxy emerged when King James II, who came to the English throne in 1685, annulled the colonial charters and merged all the New England colonies, which eventually included New York and New Jersey, into the Dominion of New England and appointed Sir Edmund Andros governor of the province in May of 1686. Andros, whom Charles II had appointed royal governor of New York in 1674, had already attempted to assert his authority over the lands west of the Connecticut River, which involved a confrontation with Captain Thomas Bull at Saybrook. However, it was not until the creation of the Dominion that Andros finally had the royal authority and backing to impose his will on the settlements of New England.

In spite of the popular story that Connecticut defied the royal order and hid the colony's charter in the hollow part of an oak tree on Samuel Wyllys's property—in what thereafter became known as the "Charter Oak"—the truth is that Connecticut did not defy the order and, as did the rest of the colonies in New England, submitted to the royal governor for the next two years. Only after news of the Glorious Revolution in England had reached the shores of North America did New Englanders defy the order, seizing and imprisoning Andros on April 18, 1689, and reasserting their right to self-rule. Connecticut and New Haven, following the example of Massachusetts, reorganized themselves according to the charter of 1662. In 1693, the colony sent Fitz-John Winthrop, the son of John Winthrop Jr. to England, where King William and Queen Mary approved the colony's charter and pre-Dominion government. Rhode Island did the same, but Massachusetts was unable to reclaim its old charter and received a new one in 1691, making it a royal colony. Like Rhode Island, Connecticut was without a royal governor for the remainder of the colonial period and, instead of writing a state constitution during the American Revolution, it simply retained its old charter until making serious revisions in 1818.

According to the story of the Charter Oak, Andros, with his council and 30 to 60 armed men, arrived in Hartford on October 31, 1687. He had come "to receive . . . the surrender of [the] Charter," and having arrived while the General Assembly was still in session, he was forced to wait until after sunset before the charter was brought into the room. It was taken out of its long mahogany box and placed on the table. The story has a few variant versions hereafter, but all agree that the candles were extinguished and in the darkness and confusion, the charter was taken and passed through an open window to Captain Joseph Wadsworth, who then hid it in the hollow part of an oak tree on the Wyllys estate. The charter, now hanging in the Museum of Connecticut History in Hartford, remained there until May 1689, when it was returned to the State House, and the oak tree on the Wyllys estate became a sacred, historical site until a lightning storm destroyed it on August 21, 1856.

The Glorious Revolution of 1688 brought many changes to both the British Isles and North America. Firstly, a bill of rights ensured Parliament's supremacy and gave rise to the Whig Party in both Britain and the colonies. This was followed by the Toleration Act of 1689, a limited guarantee of toleration for Protestant dissenters (at least those who believed in the Trinity). In New England, where settlers had built Bible commonwealths while adhering to the strict precepts of Calvinist theology, the question of religious toleration had profound and lasting effects on the Puritan establishment. Except for Rhode Island, where a measure of religious toleration had existed since Roger Williams founded Providence in 1636, New Englanders generally did not tolerate dissenting sects; now, with the Toleration Act, they were required to tolerate Anglicans as well as Quakers, Baptists, and other dissenting Protestants. Puritan conservatives, especially those in New Haven and Connecticut, grew alarmed at this new development and, as we shall see in the next chapter, took steps to prevent the demise of their godly kingdoms.

Chapter Two

CONTINUITY AND THE ROAD TO INDEPENDENCE

By the end of the seventeenth century—following New Haven's absorption into the Connecticut colony and the passing of the Toleration Act by Parliament—conservatives in New Haven and the rest of New England perceived a serious decline in religious orthodoxy and acted accordingly. Each plantation responded to its own set of circumstances, but used the events of the age, whether natural or man-made, to underscore the downward spiral of true religion. Epidemics, fires, shipwrecks, Indian wars, Stuart colonial policy, and the Half-Way Covenant were all signs of religious declension. Across New England, conservatives alluded to these events as God's anger and judgment on a wayward people.

With the rise of heterodoxy in New England, the Connecticut legislature in 1708 approved a synod of twelve ministers and four laymen to meet at Saybrook and develop the standards for the reorganization of the congregational churches. At the synod, the ministers composed the Saybrook Platform, a 15-article proclamation creating regional consociations of churches to oversee local congregations and regional associations of ministers with the authority to examine ministerial candidates on doctrine and morals. Designed to ensure greater doctrinal purity and discipline in the Connecticut churches, the Platform marked a significant shift away from the Congregationalism of the first settlers to the more unified structure of Presbyterianism and served as Connecticut's religious constitution for the remainder of the colonial period.

Despite Governor Gurdon Saltonstall and the Assembly's attempt to bring greater unity and moral discipline among the Connecticut churches, not all the counties adhered to the articles. New London County renounced them; Fairfield County, which had experienced a decline in piety and discipline, adhered to them in a strict way; New Haven County adhered to them as little as possible. Overall, though, the town of New Haven accepted the new church discipline; the Reverend James Pierpont of the First Church, after all, was a leading member at the synod and it was he, according to tradition, who was responsible for drafting "The Articles for the Administration of Church Discipline."

Although the Platform, in accordance with the Toleration Act of 1689, permitted Protestant sects outside of the congregational establishment to worship and govern themselves independently, it simultaneously required all dissenters to pay the mandatory taxes to the congregational churches. In New Haven this meant that residents were expected to pay for the support of

Pierpont's First Church, which was the sole church in New Haven until divisions caused by the religious revivals of the 1730s and 1740s led to the establishment of another church on the corner of Church and Elm Streets.

Another conservative response to the rise of heterodoxy, which might have occurred sooner if the colony had thrived as a commercial center, was the founding of a small college to prepare young men "for public employments in church and civil state." Although there had been earlier attempts at founding a college, namely by John Davenport, it was not until October 1701—when the Reverend James Pierpont of New Haven's First Church and several other ministers persuaded the Connecticut Assembly meeting in New Haven to pass an "Act for Liberty to erect a Collegiate School"—that the first Connecticut college received its charter.

However, the founding of the "Collegiate School," what would become the third oldest university in the United States, is not a simple story. It extends to the Massachusetts Bay Colony where conservative Congregationalists, including Samuel Sewall and the Mather family, were complaining about Harvard's growing heterodoxy and assisted the Connecticut Congregationalists in the founding of their own college. Although the college charter of 1701, which seems to have been partly drafted by Judge Sewall, stated that the college would prepare young men for church and state, the main intention of the founders was to create an orthodox ministry, "to Educate Persons, for the Ministry of the Churches, commonly called Presbyterian or Congregational," as President Thomas Clap later maintained. Or as the charter itself introduced the founding:

> Whereas several well disposed, and Publick spirited Persons of their sincere Regard to and Zeal for upholding and Propagating of the Christian Protestant Religion by a succession of Learned and Orthodox men have expressed by Petition their earnest desires that full Liberty and Priveledge be granted unto certain Undertakers for the founding, suitably endowing and ordering a Collegiate School within his Majesties Colony of Connecticut . . .

According to the charter, the trustees (ten in number but soon increased to eleven) had to be ministers and, looking after the affairs of the college, they later maintained their independence as a corporation from the Connecticut legislature. The board of ministers also ensured the Calvinist nature of the college by imposing tests on college officers. After Rector Timothy Cutler and the college tutor defected to Anglicanism in 1722, for example, the trustees established a requirement that all college officers subscribe to the Confession of Faith as set down in the Saybrook Platform and, in 1753, the president (who had taken over the rector's office after the incorporation of Yale in 1745) was directed to hold regular services in the college hall. Strong delcarations were adopted, ensuring the college's committment and adherence to the standards of the Westminister Confession and Saybrook Platform.

New Haven

The college prospered and expanded throughout the eighteenth century, but its location at New Haven was a later development. At the end of September of 1701, less than a month before its official founding, the interested parties had gathered at the Reverend Samuel Russell's house in Branford, choosing New Haven as the site. However, when the trustees met at Saybrook in November, they chose Saybrook to be the official site of the college, and appointed the Reverend Abraham Pierson of Killingworth (now Clinton) as rector. Although the official location of the college was now at Saybrook, where the commencements were to be held each year, the classes were nonetheless held at Pierson's parish in Killingworth, where the rector attended to his congregation. Saybrook remained the official site of the college until October 17, 1716, when the trustees voted to have it moved to its new location at New Haven *(see illustration on page 67)*.

By the beginning of the eighteenth century, New Haven was still a small agricultural town, yet it had grown in relation to other settlements in New England. Its estates were valued at £17,844, having grown from £15,402 in 1669; shortly after the college was moved to New Haven, it was valued at £28,316. With its expansion, the town became the co-capital of the colony in 1701, sharing the meetings of the Connecticut General Assembly with Hartford, a position New Haven maintained until the second half of the nineteenth century. In 1717, the new State and County Courthouse was built on the northwest side of the Green, and soon afterwards the first college building was built on the southwest corner opposite the Green, on the present-day site of Bingham Hall, marking what is today the old part of the college. On the other side of Chapel Street, the college president's house was built in 1722, a fine wooden structure in its day. So when the Connecticut legislature voted to move the college to New Haven in 1716, it was in keeping with the growth and prosperity of the town during the first half of the eighteenth century *(see illustration on page 68)*.

Other Connecticut towns, however, had claims on the college, resulting in a two-year controversy that divided the students' loyalties among their tutors in Saybrook, Wethersfield, and New Haven. The Wethersfield faction, under the tutor Elisha Williams, together with the trustees Timothy Woodbridge and Thomas Buckingham, wanted the college moved to Hartford. In 1717, the Connecticut legislature even declared Middletown to be the best location for the college. The controversy continued until the fall of 1718 when a majority vote in the Assembly, together with Governor Gurdon Saltonstall's influence, settled the matter in New Haven's favor. That same year, Elihu Yale, a descendent of one the town's original founders, gave a gift to the college of 417 books, a portrait of George I, and the royal coat of arms (worth just over £550). Consequently, the trustees named the "Collegiate School" after him, calling it "Yale College."

Upon a tombstone at Wrexham, Wales, the following lines commemorate the life of Yale's benefactor, who died three years after his gift:

Continuity and the Road to Independence

Born in America, in Europe bred,
In Africa traveled and in Asia wed,
Where long he lived and thrived: in London dead.
Much good, some ill he did, so hope's all even,
And that his soul through mercy's gone to heaven.
You that survive, and read this tale, take care
For this most certain exit to prepare,
Where blest in peace the actions of the just
Smell sweet and blossom in the silent dust.

Interestingly enough, there is no mention of the small college in New Haven, and so we must turn to the words of Cotton Mather, soliciting Yale in England to send money for the continuation of the college, where we find a more fitting and lasting epithet for an American native: "And your munificence might easily obtain for you a commemoration and perpetuation of your valuable name which indeed would be much better than an Egyptian pyramid."

One of Yale's first graduates was Jonathan Edwards (B.A. 1720; M.A. 1722), who served as a college tutor before being ordained at the parish in Northampton, Massachusetts *(see illustration on page 69)*. Edwards's significance extends beyond his *alma mater*, as he became a prominent apologist for the religious revivals sweeping across America during the 1730s and 1740s. In New England the Great Awakening, as most historians have referred to it, resulted in the emergence of a faction called the "New Lights," who, perceiving the laxity of morals and piety, opposed the disciplinary regulations of the New England churches. The old Calvinists, who were called the "Old Lights," saw these emotional revivals as dangerously anti-establishment, challenging the authority of the educated clergy. They were "unlearned, common, labouring men" and "Apostates," as the Reverend Joseph Fish commented. The New Lights, on the other hand, saw the Old Lights as overly rationalistic, whose experience with God was an impersonal one, and consequently placed a much greater emphasis on piety and the conversion experience. They moreover employed itinerant preaching as a means of converting souls, establishing inter-colonial networks and associations.

In 1721, the first revival occurred in the town of Windham, Connecticut, but it was fleeting and temporary. The main phase of the Great Awakening did not occur until the early 1730s, and after subsiding and reappearing in the early 1740s, it engulfed much of Connecticut and the rest of New England, dividing numerous congregations and towns along the lines of New and Old Lights. New Haven remained relatively conservative, especially when compared to the towns in the eastern half of Connecticut, but it too had its adherents. Three parties emerged in the town itself: the Old Lights, led by James Pierpont and later by Joseph Noyes; the moderate New Lights, who took the *via media*; and the radical New Lights, led at first by the emotionally unstable James Davenport, the great-great-grandson of the town's founder. Jonathan Edwards accompanied the young charismatic English itinerant George Whitefield on his tour of Connecticut in October 1740. The two men stopped at New Haven, where Whitefield preached an impassioned sermon and won over many moderate New Lights, who found the exhortations of James Davenport too boisterous and extravagant for their liking.

But perhaps Whitefield's words themselves are more revealing about New Haven at this time, for after preaching a sermon at the college, he remarked that at Yale, as at Harvard, "Light is become darkness." As for the New England clergy, they were lost souls: "I am verily persuaded, the Generality of Preachers talk of an unknown, unfelt Christ. And the reason why congregations have become so dead, is because dead men preach to them."

Whitefield's "dead" clergy and congregations were more noticeable in the western part of Connecticut; along the southeastern coast more than 30 separate congregational churches emerged as a result of the revivals. New Haven County and the western part of Connecticut, however, were still susceptible to the revivals, and the Old Lights, perceiving the danger of more inner-congregational splits, had the Connecticut legislature pass a series of laws to curb the excesses of the Awakening. During the 1740s itinerant preaching was banned, New Lights were fined and imprisoned, public officials were kept out or removed from office, a New Light school was closed in New London, and New Light students were expelled from Yale. The Old Lights also had the legislature state in unequivocal language that the toleration clause of the Saybrook Platform was a provision designed for sects outside of the congregational order and its Presbyterian structure, a far cry from Governor Roger Wolcott's claim in 1752 that all Protestants in Connecticut enjoy "equal Liberty."

Such maneuvering by the Old Light faction, however, had little effect on New Haven and the rest of the colony. By 1742, the First Church of New Haven was split and, after some tactical delays, the Connecticut legislature granted the New Light separatists the right to build their own church edifice. At the same time the legislature prohibited the separatists from building a church on the Green, so they built it on the corner of Church and Elm Streets and painted the wooden structure an azure blue. Thereafter it was called the "Blue Meeting-house" and later the "White Haven Church" (perhaps an amalgamation of "Whitefield" and "New Haven").

By the second half of the eighteenth century, religious uniformity in New Haven had broken down. The White Haven Church had its own schism, resulting in the founding of the Fair Haven Church. Other religious sects emerged too. In 1752, there were enough Anglicans to warrant a minister and the purchase of a piece of land for worship near the corner of Chapel and Church Streets. Two years later Trinity Church— where George Washington was to worship on his presidential tour of New England—was built and became the center of Anglican worship until it was relocated in 1816 to its present site on the Green.

Continuity and the Road to Independence

With the conclusion of the French and Indian War, Catholicism also found its way to New Haven. Several Acadian families, having settled in New Haven, were worshipping, as Ezra Stiles pointed out, "according to Roman Ritual." Since religious toleration as set down in the Toleration Act and Saybrook Platform failed to recognize non-Protestant sects, New Haven Catholics were not allowed to build a church and it was not until the influx of Irish workers for the Farmington Canal that Christ's Church was built in 1834 on the corner of York Street and Davenport Avenue.

Another non-Protestant sect to make inroads in New Haven during the second half of the eighteenth century was Judaism. In the summer of 1772, a Jewish family from Venice settled in New Haven and was worshipping at home according to the Jewish faith. Although two Portuguese brothers of the Jewish faith had come to New Haven at some earlier date, they had, as Ezra Stiles remarked, "renounced Judaism and all religion," dating the first official worship of Judaism in New Haven to the eve of the American Revolution.

Certain historians have drawn parallels between the Great Awakening and the American Revolution. Its anti-authoritarianism and inter-colonial networks provided the first steps, as some historians have thought, toward a united front against the British government and its colonial policies. The history of the American Revolution is of course more complicated than drawing direct parallels to the Great Awakening, but when it comes to the history of New Haven and Connecticut, there are indeed noticeable parallels between religion and politics; that is, between the New Light faction and the Patriot cause.

When the Old Lights, who were controlling the political offices of the Connecticut towns and legislature, acted against the New Lights during the 1740s, they unintentionally gave rise to a new political faction, which sought public offices and the overthrow of the conservative hegemony. For the next 20 years, a political struggle ensued between the factions; the New Lights gradually gained public appointments and offices. Indeed, by 1760, a year after the New Lights' unsuccessful attempt to prevent Thomas Fitch's reelection to the governorship, the Reverend Samuel Johnson told the Archbishop of Canterbury that the New Lights were gaining support in the lower house of the Connecticut Assembly, and that they were still trying to remove "the governor and several of the upper house for not favouring them." The New Lights failed again, but by 1763 they were, according to William Samuel Johnson, "nearly the ruling part of the government," and they had managed to do so by giving more attention "to civil affairs" and by "the close union among themselves in politics."

With the conclusion of the French and Indian War, the British government attempted to have the colonies pay a part of the large war debt and the rising costs of administering an extensive empire by passing the Sugar Act in 1764, the Stamp Act in 1765, and the Townshend Act in 1767. The faction associated with the New Lights in Connecticut opposed these new taxes and won the popular support of the people. Although both factions generally opposed the taxes imposed by Parliament, the Old Light faction was more ready to accept the supremacy of Parliament and did not question its right to tax the colonies on constitutional grounds. As Governor Fitch, of the Old Light faction, told colonial agent Richard Jackson on the eve of the Stamp Act, if that

> supreme . . . [body] . . . in their superior wisdom shall judge it expedient to and accordingly do pass an act for laying those Burdens upon us we must submit. We never pretend in the least to question whether acts of Parliament expressly extended to the plantations are binding but always submit to them as binding.

The Reverend Chauncey Whittelsey of the Old Light First Church of New Haven equally acquiesced to Parliament's authority over the colonies. "What we can't avoid, we must bear," he told Ezra Stiles. This "duty (if laid) is laid by the Parliament of Great Britain: it must therefore be wise and right and best."

The New Lights, however, were less understanding and took a lead role in the movement to repeal the tax, especially in the eastern part of Connecticut, where the New Light movement had its origins and strongest support, and where the "Sons of the Liberty" were about to emerge as opponents of the stamp duty and eventually of British colonial rule itself. In the eastern towns of New London, Norwich, Lebanon, and Windham, the new stamp-master was burned in effigy. In West Haven, a "giant" effigy of a "horrible Monster" was placed on a horse, led out of town "with the discordant Noise of Drums, Fiddles, and taunting Huzzas," and condemned at a mock trial "as an unjust Intruder, a Patron of Ignorance, a Fore of English Freedom, etc., and was sentenced to be burnt." This protest was conducted in a more orderly fashion than in the east, but even the towns of western Connecticut, including New Haven, were up in arms at the new tax.

In New Haven, Naphtali Daggett and John Hubbard, both of the New Light faction, opposed the Stamp Act and insisted that it be repealed. In fact, both factions in New Haven opposed the tax. Even Jared Ingersoll—an Old Light resident who had served as Connecticut's colonial agent in London before accepting the office of stamp-master for Connecticut—had opposed the tax. As part of the Old Light faction, however, Ingersoll accepted Parliament's supreme authority and predicted that the colonists would do the same when Parliament passed the bill on March 22, 1765. What is more, he predicted that the colonists would prefer a native tax collector to a foreign one and secured the office of stamp distributor for Connecticut on the advice of his trusted friend Benjamin Franklin, who was also serving as a colonial agent at the time. Like Franklin, Ingersoll had not fathomed the depth of colonial resentment against the tax; therefore, after returning to Connecticut in 1765, he was received as a traitor by many of his fellow countrymen. In the August 9 issue of the *Connecticut Gazette*, edited and published in New Haven by Benjamin Franklin's nephew Benjamain Mecom, the New Light Naphtali Daggett welcomed the stamp-master home with the following rebuke:

Those who have lately set themselves up for Patriots and boasted a generous Love for their Country, as they are now saying (O Disgrace to Humanity!) are THEY now creeping after the Profits of collecting the unrighteous American Stamp-Duty? . . . But had you not rather these Duties should be collected by your Brethren, than by Foreigners? No! vile Miscreant! Indeed we had not. . . . You are to look for Nothing but the hatred and detestation of all the Good and the Virtuous.

In the first week of September, a New Haven mob met outside of Ingersoll's house and demanded his resignation. When the stamp-master replied that he did not know if he had "the power" to do so because he had accepted the office in person, the mob demanded that he hand over the stamps when they arrived "in Order to make a Bon Fire—or have his house pull'd down." Ingersoll then asked that they be patient and wait until the next meeting of the General Assembly when he would receive his orders and they would make their remonstrance known. Soon afterwards the crowd dispersed, but only after Ingersoll had promised that when the stamps arrived in New Haven he would either send them back to England or "when they were in his House, his Doors should be open, and they would then act as they thought proper."

Compared to the riots in Boston and Newport a week earlier, and the disturbances in townships of eastern Connecticut, the protests at New Haven were relatively calm and orderly. Nonetheless, they were defiant and vituperative. His initials, as it was pointed out in public, were the same as Judas Iscariot. And at the September 17 town meeting in which Roger Sherman and Samuel Bishop were chosen deputies to represent New Haven at the special session of the General Assembly (to meet at Hartford on September 19), the town's freemen instructed the representatives to do their best at this session and the following one in New Haven to bring about repeal. They then proceeded to put forward another resolution calling for Ingersoll's immediate resignation, to which the stamp-master replied that he "would NOT resign till he discover[ed] how the General Assembly were inclined in that Respect."

When the legislature finally convened on September 19, Ingersoll was stopped on his way to Hartford by an angry mob of about 500 men, mainly from the counties of New London and Windham and members of the Sons of Liberty. They demanded his resignation and, after a brief protest, he was forced to resign his office and join them in "three Cheers for Liberty and property." The men, whose numbers had now grown to about 1,000, escorted the former stamp-master to Hartford where he read his resignation out loud within hearing distance of the General Assembly.

On November 1, the day the stamp tax was to take effect, the bells of the New Haven State House, First Church, and Yale College tolled as an act of mourning. Captain Wolcott, with a large crowd, buried a coffin containing the Stamp Act while the king's colors fluttered in the wind above the grave. The town officials, including those in the legal profession, refused to comply with the tax and simply did not conduct business that required the official use of the stamps. The Custom House suspended its transactions until the end of December when the pressures of the merchant class forced New Haven officials to clear ships using unstamped paper. Certain merchants had nonetheless been involved in smuggling activities, including the soon-to-be-infamous Benedict Arnold, who led an angry mob against an apparent informant and ran him out of town.

Something had to be done, and on February 3, 1766, a town meeting was called to deal with the Stamp Act crisis directly. The freemen reached a consensus—by a vote of 274 to 1—that the Stamp Act was "unconstitutional" and "not binding on the Conscience" of the people. With the change of ministry in London, repeal of the Stamp Act passed through Parliament on March 18; news of it reached New Haven by way of Boston on May 19. The *Connecticut Gazette* of New Haven reported the event: "In the morning, small arms were fired in the streets, cannons roared, bells tolled, and the clergy gave public thanks; in the evening, there was a bonfire and dancing."

Shortly before news of the repeal had reached New Haven, the New Light faction defeated the conservatives in the election of 1766 and took control of the colonial legislature. The Sons of Liberty, having met at Hartford in late March, put forward their candidates to defeat Governor Fitch and his four assistants, considered to be not very strong "patriots to the republick." By May 12, William Pitkin Sr. of the New Light faction had defeated Fitch to become governor, and Jonathan Trumbull, also of the New Light faction, was elected lieutenant governor *(see illustration on page 69)*. The four assistants were likewise defeated by the New Light interest, and in the elections that followed the New Lights continued to dominate the Assembly.

The Stamp Act was the determining factor behind this dramatic shift in Connecticut politics; as the Old Light Benjamin Gale complained the following year, the election of 1767 was lost because of "N[ew] Light, St[amp] Act, and Satan." The Stamp Act also paved the way for American independence from the mother country. Gale remarked shortly after the tax was repealed, "The Stamp Act has laid the foundations for America being an Independent State," and said that for years to come there would be "a Period of Slaughter and Blood."

With the repeal of the Stamp Act, Parliament issued the Declaratory Act, which paved the way for the Townshend Act of 1767 and Tea Act of 1773, and eventually the American Declaration of Independence. New Haven's participation in the patriotic cause during this period included non-importation and similar acts of defiance. At a town meeting in 1769, freemen decided "it is expedient for the Town to take all prudent and legal Measures to encourage the Produce and Manufactures of this Colony, and to lessen the Use of Superfluities, and more especially . . . articles imported from aboard."

Seniors at Yale College supported the boycott by voting to wear homespun cloth at the Commencement of 1768–1769. At the Commencement of 1774, two Yale candidates for the degree of M.A. presented their arguments for "The Rights of Americans" and the "Unconstitutional Measures of the British Parliament."

When the British government passed the Boston Port Act in response to the Boston Tea Party, New Haven, like most colonial towns, voted to support the inhabitants of Boston and observe the acts of non-intercourse and non-importation drawn up by the first Continental Congress. Committees of correspondence and inspection were established, but when the first shots were fired at Lexington, New Haven called a town meeting and—acting a few days before the Connecticut legislature sent military aid to the Boston insurgents under the command Colonel Israel Putnam—voted to do nothing.

This conservative victory, however, did not please everyone. Benedict Arnold, who had recently been appointed captain of the "Second Company of the Governor's Guard," summoned his men together and proposed that they march to the aid of the Boston insurgents. Fifty of the 64 militiamen agreed and reenlisted as volunteers. The next day they were drilling on the Green, where they received the blessing of the New Light minister Jonathan Edwards Jr. of the White Haven Church. Assembling at the corner of College and Chapel Streets in front of Beers's tavern, Captain Arnold told his men that the town authorities had ignored his request for the keys to the powder house at the top of the hill of what is today Prospect Street. He then ordered Lieutenant Jesse Leavenworth to demand the keys from the selectmen who were now meeting at the tavern with the Committee of Safety, and to inform them that if the keys were "not forthcoming within five minutes, my men will break into the supply-house and help themselves." This time the selectmen conceded to Arnold's request and the company marched to Boston, where it joined the ranks of the Continental Army. Some of the men, including Arnold, joined the expedition against Ticonderoga at Lake Champlain and the failed siege of Quebec City; some joined other contingents, and the remainder returned to New Haven a month later, where they greeted General George Washington on July 2, 1775, en route to take command of his army in Massachusetts.

Captain Arnold was soon promoted to the rank of brigadier and then major general, and distinguished himself heroically at the battle of Saratoga. However, he soon defected to the Loyalist side and, in a final act of betrayal, led a British invasion against New London, not far from his birthplace in Norwich. He eventually fled to England, where he spent the remainder of his life dejected and penitent.

Other New Haveners proved to be more steadfast. David Wooster, a Yale graduate and veteran commander of the French and Indian War, was commissioned a major general in the Connecticut militia at the beginning of the war. Soon thereafter, he was captured by the British at the battle of Quebec City, then exchanged as a prisoner of war shortly afterwards. Two years later, while heroically defending the town of Danbury from a British invasion, he received a mortal wound and died on the field rallying his troops near Ridgefield *(see illustration on page 70)*.

David Humphreys, another Yale graduate and man of many talents, was appointed General Washington's aide-de-camp at the beginning of the war and formed a close friendship with the general, earning the appellation "the belov'd of Washington." He was also a diplomat, merchant, poet, and historian, and his military service extended to the War of 1812. On February 21, 1818, he died suddenly from an organic disease of the heart and was buried in the New Haven Grove Street Cemetery, where the following inscription (translated from the original Latin) by his friend John Trumbull, the author of *M'Fingal*, bears testimony to his life:

> David Humphreys, doctor of laws, member of the Academy of Sciences of Philadelphia, Massachusetts, and Connecticut, of the Bath [Agricultural Society] and of the Royal Society of London. Fired with the love of country and of liberty, he consecrated his youth wholly to the service of the republic, which he defended by his arms, aided by his counsels, adorned by his learning, and preserved in harmony with foreign nations. In the field he was the companion and aid of the great Washington, a colonel in the army of his country, and commander of the veteran volunteers of Connecticut. He went as an ambassador to the courts of Portugal and Spain, and, returning, enriched his native land with the true golden fleece [Humphreys introduced merino sheep from Spain to the United States]. He was a distinguished historian and poet; a model and a patron of science, and of the ornamental and useful arts. After a full discharge of every duty, and a life well spent, he died on the 21st day of February, 1818, aged sixty-five years.

Although New Haven, as a seaport town, did not obtain the strategic importance of Boston, New York, Philadelphia, and Charleston during the Revolutionary War, it did participate in the action and eventually fell victim to the ravages and spoliation of war. With the British invasions of Connecticut in 1777, the British forces had launched a few small raids along the coastline of New Haven County, striking at Sachem's Head in June, Milford Farms in August, and Guilford in December. This was likely in response to an earlier raid by the Americans against the British at Sag Harbor, Long Island, in May of that same year, when Lieutenant Colonel Return Jonathan Meigs, having learned that the enemy had a supply of military stores at Sag Harbor guarded by no more than 100 men, led an expedition from New Haven harbor. With 13 whaleboats, he left the harbor on May 23 and, after collecting reinforcements at Guilford, crossed the Sound from Sachem's Head with about 170 men. The expedition was protected by two armed sloops, and included another unarmed one to carry prisoners back to Connecticut. Within 25 hours, Colonel Meigs returned the next day with no loss of American life, having destroyed enemy vessels and supplies and taken about 90 prisoners. One American soldier, Christopher Vail of Shouthold, recalled the event in his journal:

While at New Haven we had information that a body of refugees about one hundred in number was at Saggharbour on a foraging party with one armed brig of 14 guns, and 13 coasting vessels in order to carry away what was collected. Their business being about completed, and ready to depart when the information was given. Immediately Col. Meigs provided a number of whale boats and proceeded with our force for Long Island. We arrived at a place on the north side of the Island called Bailey's beach which was 14 miles from Saggharbour. The afternoon following at this place the carrying place was about 40 rods over. Here we took our boats by hand and carried them across and put them into a creek called Mill Creek. From this place it was about 2 or 3 hours rowing to Saggharbour. In the first part of the night we rowed across the bay and came to a neck of sand which was about 4 rods wide to the water on the other side which led to Sag harbour, and here we again took up our boats and carried them across this isthmus and again embarked, at this time about one mile from the enemy. We landed on the west of the port about half a mile and surrounded the village at once and proceeded down to their quarters where we completely succeeded in capturing the whole force except one man. We burnt all the coasting vessels which was all loaded and laid along side the wharf and a store that was 60 feet long that stood on the wharf. It so happened that they had completed all their business at this place and the afternoon before they had received a months pay and had a sham fight and damned the Yankies and wished them to come over for there never was a better time. Each man had a wooden flint in his musket and after their sham fight they sent the greatest villan belonging to their gang to Southampton to engage a dinner for the whole company the next day on their march up the Island. They remained went to drinking &c. and all got pretty well boozey. When we arrived we took ninety nine Tories. Some had nothing but his shirt on, some a pair of trowsers others perhaps 1 stocking and one shoe and in fact they were carried off in their situation to New Haven, and none escaped except the armed brig which was anchored off and the men spoken of above. The whole of the time our troops was there the brig was firing broadsides in every direction. We returned back to New Haven . . . with our gentry where they were all deposited in the town gaol.

New Haven had not been attacked during the early phase of the war, but on July 5, 1779, when the town was planning to celebrate the third anniversary of independence, the British launched a full invasion. (New Haven was celebrating the anniversary a day after the actual declaration of independence so as not to break the Sabbath.) As 48 vessels under the command of Sir George Collier containing about 3,000 British, Hessian, and Tory soldiers sailed up the Sound and anchored off West Haven in the early hours of the morning, a cannon sounded the first alarm. At about 5 a.m., President Ezra Stiles climbed the stairs of the Yale College Athenaeum with a spy-glass and spotted "the boats pulling off from the ships and landing a little after sunrise."

New Haven

About 1,500 troops under the command of Brigadier General Garth came ashore at West Haven, and another contingent of troops under the command of Major General William Tryon came ashore at East Haven at about 10 a.m. Garth's troops landed with little resistance at Savin Rock and rested on the West Haven Green, giving Tyron's contingent time to land near Lighthouse Point and capture Black Rock Fort and Beacon Hill before advancing in a two-prong attack toward New Haven (see illustration on page 71).

Loyalist Yale graduates Colonel Edmund Fanning and William and Thomas Chandler accompanied the British, serving as their guides while a number of other New Haven Loyalists greeted the British after they landed in West and East Haven. Like most civil wars, town allegiances varied and were capable of dividing families and friends. John Adams once alluded to this Patriot-Loyalist divide when he recalled that on the eve of the Revolution, one-third of the colonists were Loyalists, one-third Patriots, and the remainder indifferent. New Haven, too, was divided on the question of loyalty; President Ezra Stiles later remarked on the invasion of New Haven: "One third of the population armed and went to meet the enemy. A quarter moved out of town and the rest, Tories and timid Whigs, remained unmoved."

Among those who sought safety in the countryside were Stiles's two daughters. He sent them to Cheshire, to the house of the Reverend John Foote, while others sought safety in Hamden, North Haven, and Wallingford. Some of those who fled to the houses of relatives and friends close to West Rock climbed the great rock to see the British advance to Thompson's Bridge, describing it as both striking and beautiful. In this flight, there were even some humorous episodes. Timothy Atwater, for example, was returning from the fields after hearing the alarm gun and met a woman hurrying out of town with a cat in her arms. Acquainted with the woman, he asked her by name, "Why, Mrs. ——, what is the matter?"

"The British are coming," she exclaimed in a terrible state.

"But where are your children?" he inquired.

"Why, at home, I suppose."

"Well," said Mr. Atwater, "hadn't you better go back and get them, and leave the cat?"

"Perhaps I had," she said and returned to town.

While a number of women and children fled into the countryside, another third of the population of approximately 4,000 to 6,000 inhabitants assembled to defend New Haven against the enemy incursion. A few Yale students, with their own captain and the old professor Naphtali Daggett, accompanied Captain James Hillhouse—commander of the Foot Guards—Captain Phineas Bradley, and Lieutenant Colonel Hezekiah Sabin—commander of the Connecticut militia in the New Haven district—to the bridge on West River. "Our artillery and militia moved to West Bridge," reported Ezra Stiles, "pulled it up, and planted to make a stand." But Captain Hillhouse decided to cross the bridge and advance as far as the foot of Milford Hill, where he and his men first engaged the enemy. From the vantage point of a fence, they fired at Garth's advance party, which they then chased back to the main body of troops. The British quickly forced the New Haven militia to retreat back to their artillery position at West Bridge. Having brought down the bridge to prevent a British crossing, Captain Bradley fired his artillery at the advancing British soldiers who now sought another route across the river *(see illustration on page 72)*.

Meanwhile, 72-year-old Professor Daggett, president emeritus of the college, had taken up a position in a wooded area near Milford Hill and was firing his old fowling musket at the advancing British forces. He had ridden out to battle on his old black mare, and when Hillhouse and his men retreated, he held his position and fired at the advancing line. The young Elizur Goodrich recalled the incident in the *Annals of the American Pulpit*:

> I well remember the surprise we felt as we were marching over West Bridge towards the enemy, to see Dr. Daggett riding furiously by us on his old black mare, with his long fowling piece in his hand, ready for action. We knew the old gentleman had studied the matter thoroughly, and settled his own mind as to the right and propriety of fighting it out, but were not quite prepared to see him come forth in so gallant a style to carry his principles in practice. Giving him a hearty cheer as he passed, we turned down to West Haven at the foot of Milford Hill, while he ascended a little to the west and took his station in a copse of wood where he seemed to be reconnoitering the enemy, like one who was determined to bide his time. As we passed on toward the south we met an advanced guard of the enemy, and taking our stand at a line of fence we fired on them several times, then chased them the length of three or four fields as they retreated, till we found ourselves involved with the main body, and in danger of being surrounded. It was now our turn to run, and we did for our lives. Passing by Dr. Daggett in his station on the hill, we retreated rapidly across West Bridge, which was instantly taken down by persons who stood ready for the purpose, to prevent the enemy from entering the town by that road.

After the American retreat, the British sent out a party to subdue the sniper in the copse of wood and were surprised to find an old man with an old, antiquated fowling musket. "What are you doing there, you old fool," inquired the British officer, "firing on his Majesty's troops?"

"Exercising the rights of war," said Daggett.

"If I let you go this time, you rascal," asked the officer, "will you ever fire again on the troops of his Majesty?"

"Nothing more likely," responded Daggett in his audacious and droll way. The corollary was that the old professor received a beating, his shoes were removed, and he was forced to march barefoot. His beating later included a stab wound and there can be no doubt that his death 16 months later was partly due to the brutal treatment he had received at the hands of his captors.

New Haven

Daggett recalled the incident in a sworn account 21 days later, now preserved at the office of the Secretary of State in Hartford:

> One of them gave me four gashes on my head with the edge of his bayonet, to the skull-bone, which caused a plentiful effusion of blood. The other gave me three slight pricks with the point of his bayonet on the trunk of my body, but they were no more than skin deep. But what is a thousand times worse . . . is the blows and bruises they gave me with the heavy barrels of their guns on my bowels . . . , by which bruises I have been confined to my bed ever since. . . . They then bade me march toward the main body which was about twelve rods distance.
>
> [After further insults and robbery,] They drove me with the main body a hasty march of five miles or more. I was insulted in the most shocking manner by the ruffian soldiers, many of which came at me with fixed bayonets, and swore they would kill me on the spot. They damned me, those that took me, because they spared my life. Thus, amid a thousand insults, my infernal drivers hastened me along, faster than my strength would admit in the extreme heat of the day, weakened as I was by my wounds and the loss of blood, which, at a moderate computation, could not be less than one quart. And when I failed, in some degree, through faintness, he would strike me on the back with a heavy walking-staff, and kick me behind with his foot. At length, by the supporting power of God, I arrived at the Green, New Haven. But my life was almost spent, the world around me several times appearing as dark as midnight. I obtained leave of an officer to be carried into the Widow Lyman's and laid upon a bed, where I lay the rest of the day and succeeding night, in such acute and excruciating pain as I never felt before.

War will always bring out the worst in men and there is perhaps no better test of a man's true character than how he behaves under the stresses and hardships of warfare. One soldier, therefore, who deserves special mention during the invasion of New Haven is British Adjutant William Campbell. While the British were resting at the West Haven Green, he had come to the rescue of the patriotic minister Mr. Williston, who had broken a leg while attempting to escape. Williston was now receiving threats of death and rough treatment from a group of West Haven Tories. Campbell intervened, saying "we make war on soldiers, not civilians," and had the parson carried into his house.

After having provided for his care, Campbell ordered the regiment's surgeon to set the broken limb while he returned to the Green, where he had British looters arrested for destroying property. He then joined the British advance and—at about the same time as Daggett's capture—ascended Milford Hill either to communcate with the flanking party on that side or to get a better view of the countryside. A young Patriot sniper named Johnson, who had lingered behind after the retreat, took careful aim and shot the British officer through the chest, close to the heart. The officer fell mortally wounded by the side of the road and was carried to a house on the south side of the road, where he died attended by his servant. The next day the locals carried him upon a sheep-litter, wrapped in a blanket, and buried him in a shallow, unmarked grave close to the spot where he had fallen. For years they spoke of his kindness to the Reverend Williston. In 1831, John Warner Barber, the engraver, historian, and author of *Connecticut Historical Collections*, marked the site with a rough stone bearing Campbell's name and the date of his death *(see illustration on page 72)*. Vandals destroyed the monument 41 years later, but eventually the road on which he had been mortally wounded became known as Campbell Avenue and, in 1891, the New Haven Colony Historical Society replaced the stone in an elaborate ceremony. On August 19, 2001, the town of West Haven, in remembrance of Adjutant William Campbell's kindness, rededicated the gravesite by founding a small park on the site around the stone.

The British, unable to cross at West Bridge, marched northward to Derby Road, where they crossed at Thompson's Bridge below West Rock, all the time receiving fire from the Hotchkissville (Westville) and Derby militiamen. The young Aaron Burr, who was in New Haven visiting his uncle Pierpont Edwards, directed these operations, while Colonel Sabin moved his men in an attempt to block the British advance down Goffe Street and Whalley Avenue. The future vice-president of the United States and Sabin slowed the advance, but the American Patriots were decidedly defeated at the junction of Dixwell and Whalley and retreated to the eastern parts of town. By noon the British were in full control of the town and many soldiers proceeded to get drunk, pillaging and terrorizing the inhabitants of New Haven. Among the defenseless casualties were Benjamin English, who was murdered in his own house; Nathan Beers Sr., who was struck down in his doorway; and Elisha Tuttle, a mentally disturbed man suffering from epilepsy, who was beaten, had his tongue cut out, and later died from his injuries.

In the meantime Tryon's troops—consisting chiefly of Hessians and Tories—had landed in two divisions near Lighthouse Point, advanced to Morris Cove, and captured Black Rock Fort (later Fort Hale) and Beacon Hill. Having received some resistance from the local militia, they routed the Patriots quite easily and proceeded to pillage the East Haven countryside.

After capturing Beacon Hill, Tyron crossed the Quinnipiac River to New Haven on Leavenworth's Ferry and attended a conference with the leading officers, which probably took place in the State House on the Green. According to tradition, the Loyalists Fanning and the Chandler brothers dissuaded the British from burning the public buildings and college during this conference, but it was more complicated than this, as the British planned to withdraw and might have had intelligence that the Patriots were reassembling in the countryside. General Tryon made the following report to Sir Henry Clinton on July 20, 1779: "The collection of the enemy in force, and with heavier cannon than our own diverted the General [Garth] from that passage [of burning the buildings]." And still Garth appears to have thought of burning the town, for the "next morning, as there was not a shot fired to molest the retreat, General Garth changed his design and destroyed only the public stores, some vessels, and ordinance."

Although the New Haven militia was forced to retreat to the northern and eastern parts of the countryside, they soon began to reorganize and assemble men from the surrounding towns and counties. Colonel Street Hall of Wallingford rode across the country shouting, "Turn out. The British are in New Haven!" Many others sounded the alarm. Those who responded were General Artemus Ward, who appeared with some Continental soldiers, and militiamen from Hamden, North Haven, Wallingford, Meriden, Derby, Guilford, and other surrounding towns. Others acted on their own free will when they heard the sound of cannon fire in the distance. In his autobiography, Lyman Beecher reported how his uncle and other men from North Guilford came to the defense of New Haven after hearing the sound of artillery in the distance:

> I remember that day we were plowing, when we heard the sound of cannon toward New Haven. "Whoa!" said Uncle Benton; stopped team, off harness, mounted old Sorrell, bareback, shouldered the old musket, and rode off to New Haven. Deacon Bartlett went too; and Sam Bartlett said he never saw his father more keen after deer than he was to get a shot at the regulars.

By nightfall about 1,000 fighting men had assembled and were ready to make a counterattack on New Haven. Lieutenant John Holbrook (whose father had advised him earlier that morning, "You are going to fight the enemies of your country; now remember that I had rather see you brought back wounded in front than in running from the enemy") made several jaunts into town. Noticing how drunk and disorderly the enemy was, he advised General Ward to make a night attack on the British. When his advice was rejected, he pleaded for a handful of men to make a surprise attack at night, but Ward remained calm and did not grant his request.

On Tuesday morning, July 6, the British troops withdrew in an orderly fashion, burning the shops on Long Wharf and encountering little resistance from General Ward's men on Beacon Hill. As they sailed back to New York City, they laid siege to Fairfield and Norwalk, burning large portions of both towns. Thus, New Haven was fortunate to have escaped with so little damage. But the fate of war is never known until after the dust has settled. As Captain Hillhouse's wife Sarah Loyd Hillhouse told her cousin in Danbury two weeks later, the siege could have been a lot worse, as when the British had attacked and burned the town of Danbury in April 1777:

> The late disagreeable visit we had from our common enemy has been the reason why I have not sooner answered your last letter. You who have gone through a like scene can easily imagine the consternation this town must be in on the occasion. However, we fared much better than we feared, as we expected nothing but to see

the town reduced to ashes. My aunt Hillhouse stayed at home, and, happening to find an officer of humanity, was treated with politeness . . . a very few were as fortunate. . . . The rest of the inhabitants were plundered and abused. . . . My feelings are not to be described. I can only tell you that Mr. Hillhouse was the first that attacked them with a very small party of men with him. Old Aunt Lucas and myself rode off when the enemy were within two miles of us. The excessive heat of the day, together with the fright, and above all the distress I felt for my best friend's safety had such an effect upon me that for some days we were all fearful of the consequences. But I am happily recovered . . .

When the dust had settled and New Haven counted its losses, there were 27 dead and 17 wounded while the British counted their losses at 9 dead and 40 wounded. Why there were more dead than wounded was explained by the *Connecticut Journal*:

> As many of our dead upon examination appear to have been wounded with shot but not mortally, and afterwards to have been killed with bayonets, this demonstrates the true reason why the number of the dead exceeded that of the living, to be, that being wounded and falling into the enemy's hands they were afterwards killed.

As for the damage to property, a town committee estimated it to be in the area of £25,000. Later the Reverend Benjamin Trumbull of North Haven, who might have included the surrounding area, placed it closer to £39,000, neither being a small sum when we consider the depreciation of paper currency at the time. By the end of the war, Trumbull also said that New Haven had lost 210 soldiers and seamen, no small number when we consider the population of the town and its surrounding borders was approximately 6,000 inhabitants.

Chapter Three

A NEW NATION AND THE ROAD TO FREEDOM

During the eighteenth century, New Haven expanded and prospered as a town and, by the end of the Revolutionary War, had become one of the important seaport towns of the United States. With peace, there were close to 8,000 inhabitants, with less than half of that number living within the limits of town itself. Yale College now had 260 undergraduates enrolled, 25 percent more than in any other American college, and was no longer listing students according to social rank. The town had eight or nine lawyers in a profession that had only recently grown in importance and was beginning to receive public recognition. A stagecoach left for Hartford every Wednesday and Saturday, one going to Springfield and the other connecting with another coach to Boston. Postal-riders carried mail to and from New York twice a week, as well as to and from Boston once a week, taking the inland route via Hartford and Springfield and the coastal route via New London and Providence *(see illustration on page 73)*.

Merchant ships also began to sail directly from Union Wharf and Long Wharf to the British Isles, and soon there were transportation vessels traveling to the southern states. However, most of New Haven's trade was still with the West Indies, so many of its seagoing vessels sailed in that direction with cargoes of horses, oxen, pork, beef, and lumber, and returning with cargoes of molasses and sugar. In the year 1784, it was recorded that New Haven had 33 seagoing vessels, the number having fallen from 40 before the war. This number can be misleading, however, since in 1781, with the cessation of hostilities at the Battle of Yorktown, New Haven had only one seagoing vessel, putting its annual growth at 1,100 percent.

New Haven's postwar economic growth was something quite astounding, especially when we consider the economic difficulties facing other towns and cities in the United States in the postwar years. Indeed, by the end of 1784 the town had close to 60 shops, including the leading retail names of Broome and Platt, Shipman, Drake, Howell, Perit, Helms, and Austin. There was also a "huge fund of mechanical skill and aptitude," which included the ingenious Amos Buell, engraver, type-founder, coiner, and goldsmith; the talented Amos Doolittle, one of America's earliest copperplate engravers, whose shop was on the west side of College Street; and Jonathan Fenton, who made eyeglasses, lenses, and telescopes, as well as an assortment of navigational and surveying instruments. The talent of these local artisans and others ensured New Haven's reputation as a leading hardware and clock-manufacturing city by the middle of the nineteenth century. Isaac Doolittle, Nathaniel Jocelyn, and Hezekiah Hotchkiss had already been making brass clocks during the colonial period, but many New Haveners would not be able to afford them until they were mass produced by Chauncey Jerome in the 1840s.

Although New Haven had no real local manufactories by the end of the war—the result of many years of British mercantilism—it quickly adapted to the industrial age and, by 1818, had one hat factory, one nail factory, one powder mill, two cotton mills, two paper mills, seventeen boot and shoe makers, and eight "chaise and wagon makers." By the early nineteenth century, carriage and wagon making became New Haven's leading manufacture and customers including Presidents Andrew Jackson and Martin Van Buren ordered their carriages or wagons from this growing manufacturing center. One of the earliest New Haven carriage makers was John Cook, who had been manufacturing two-wheeled carriages as early as 1794. Soon other firms were competing in the market, including specialist firms that made carriage parts, like Jonathan Mix who invented the elliptical steel spring. James Brewster, who opened his factory at the corner of Elm and High Streets in 1810 (later he relocated it at the end of Wooster Street), became the most prominent of these carriage makers. But it was G&D Cook & Company on State Street, between Grove and Wall, that developed the assembly line method of carriage making on the eve of the Civil War and became the first mass producer of carriages, increasing production from one to ten carriages a day. One observer captured the boon of this industry in the first half of the nineteenth century when he wrote in 1836, "There are within the city limits twelve coach making establishments; and it is estimated that the value of the carriages manufactured at present will amount to about half a million of dollars annually."

New Haven had other manufactures, including firearms, watches, textiles, rubber, paper, and tools. Carriages, springs, clocks, boots and shoes, locks, and hardware—all manufactured in or near the New Haven area—were the city's chief exports. By 1860, the city had over 215 manufactures, employing as many as 4,900 men and 3,100 women, of whom a quarter, mostly men, were making carriages and carriage parts.

One New Havener who was instrumental to this manufacturing revolution was the inventor Eli Whitney, whose cotton gin revolutionized the cotton industry in the South. A mechanically curious boy, Whitney had left his family farm in Westborough, Massachusetts to attend Yale College at the late age of 23. He graduated in 1792. Owing money to his father and needing time to prepare for the bar, he went to South Carolina to take a teaching position. When the teaching position did not materialize, Whitney opted to accompany the widow of the revolutionary hero General Nathaniel Greene to her plantation near Savannah, Georgia. There he planned to read law and assist the plantation manager Phineas Miller, another Yale alumnus, but soon his mind turned to the problem of extracting a particular genus of cotton from its seed. The sticky green seed, as many southerners knew at the time, grew inland and extracting cotton from it was more difficult than the long-staple cotton growing along the coast. With the encouragement of his patron Catherine Greene, Whitney approached the problem first by observing the hand movements of slaves and then by designing a machine to mimic those hand movements. By the summer of 1793 he had built a rather simple contraption, known as the cotton gin, which was able to separate the short-staple cotton from its sticky seed.

Yet as fate would have it, Whitney invented the cotton gin at a time when the institution of slavery was no longer profitable in the South, and speculation about its demise was increasingly put forward by both northerners and southerners. His invention, however, ensured the continuation of slavery, as increasing numbers of southern planters turned to cotton instead of tobacco. Indeed, by 1800 cotton had become the staple crop of the South, its production doubling every decade until the Civil War. Slavery was profitable once again thanks to the cotton gin, but Whitney, who had returned to the North in 1793 to obtain a patent and produce the cotton gins at his New Haven factory on Wooster and Chestnut Streets, ended up penniless. Patent laws and the pirating of the cotton gin meant that he spent much of the 1790s in southern courtrooms and did not obtain his fortune. Eventually he gave up on the South and the cotton gin and returned to the North, where he developed the foundation and techniques of what some have called the "American System of Manufacture."

Although Whitney was not the first to introduce the concept of interchangeable parts, nor the concept of using machines and dividing labor (such practices already existed in Europe), he popularized the idea of mass production in America, first in his attempt to mass produce the cotton gin, but secondly in his more successful pursuit of manufacturing firearms in the New Haven area. Having returned to the North and abandoned his cotton gin factory, Whitney received a two-year contract from the federal government in June 1798 to make 10,000 muskets; he quickly turned his mind to the manufacturing process of firearms.

In an age when gunsmiths were craftsmen and made each gun individually, the contract was exceptionally large and, furthermore, Whitney had no factory, no workers, and no experience in gun manufacturing. Yet he was both an ingenious and confident man, who thought that he could use machines to make identical and interchangeable parts while powering the factory with a milling machine. As he told Secretary of the Treasury Oliver Wolcott in the spring of 1798, "I am persuaded that Machinery moved by water adapted to this Business would greatly diminish the labor and facilitate the manufacture of this Article. Machines for forging, rolling, floating, boring, grinding, polishing, etc. may all be made use of to advantage."

Whitney began to build a firearm factory along the Hamden-New Haven border with employee housing and trained his workforce, but in the summer of 1799 he was still developing the machinery to make the interchangeable parts. He told Wolcott in July, "One of my primary objectives is to form the tools so that the tools themselves shall fashion the work and give to every part its just proportions, which once accomplished, will give exceptional uniformity to the whole." Whitney spent more time making machines than muskets and at the end of two years he still had not delivered a single musket to the government, but he had developed a new method of production whereby unskilled laborers using water-driven machines and working on a single area of production made large quantities of interchangeable parts to be assembled together.

With Thomas Jefferson's election to the U.S. presidency in 1801, Whitney extended his contract and made his first shipment that September. He did not make his final shipment until January 1809, almost 11 years after the initial contract, but he did secure his fortune and New Haven's future as a leading gun manufacturing center of the United States. In 1888, Oliver Winchester—who had formed the Winchester Repeating Arms Company in 1858 using the Whitney model—leased the old Whitney factory from the inventor's grandson to make .22-caliber rifles. He became one of New Haven's largest employers in the late nineteenth and much of the twentieth century. But Whitney's biggest contribution was his innovation of manufacturing systems, which helped to influence other New Haven manufactures, like the production of carriages, clocks, springs, hardware, rubber products, and other articles *(see illustration on page 73)*.

At about the same time Whitney was working on his cotton gin in the South, John Fitch of Windsor (present-day South Windsor) designed a steamboat, about 45 feet long, which he successfully launched on the Delaware River on August 22, 1787 in the presence of delegates from the Constitutional Convention. For 40 miles, the boat propelled itself at four miles per hour, making it the first successful launch of a steamboat in the United States. In his diary, President Ezra Stiles remarked on what one of the Connecticut delegates had seen:

> Judge Ellsworth, a member of the Federal convention, just returned from Philadelphia, visited me, and tells me the convention will not rise under three weeks. He there saw a Steam-Engine for rowing boats against the stream, invented by Sir Fitch, of Windsor, in Connecticut. He was on board the boat, and saw the experiment succeed.

Fitch went on to build several larger steamboats, including one for transporting passengers and cargo between Philadelphia and Burlington, New Jersey, but failed to resolve construction and operating costs and thereby was unable to justify the economic benefits of steam navigation. It was only after

Robert Fulton propelled his steamboat the *Clermont* up the Hudson River in August 1807 that the economic benefits of steam navigation were realized, earning Fulton the title "father of steam navigation." As steam power became more popular, the *Fulton*, the first passenger steamboat on Long Island Sound, made its first 11-hour trip from New York to New Haven in March of 1815, ushering in a new age of transportation.

The introduction of the railroad, which resulted in approximately 100 independent railroads in southern New England between 1826 and the 1880s, brought an end to the New Haven "canal craze" during the 1820s and 1830s, better known as the Farmington Canal project, an ambitious attempt to repeat the success of the Erie Canal by linking Long Island Sound with the St. Lawrence River along the Canadian border. When James Brewster and others obtained a charter from the state legislature for the Hartford and New Haven Railroad Company, they laid a track between 1833 and 1839 from New Haven to Hartford, linking the two capitals. Five years later, another charter was issued for the New York and New Haven Company and an east-west track was laid, linking New Haven and New York, which began to operate in 1846. The age of the railroad was here and, by 1872, the two companies merged to form the New York, New Haven, and Hartford Railroad Company *(see illustration on page 75)*.

With the harnessing of steam power, together with Eli Whitney's innovations in manufacturing, the city moved toward the industrial age but there was still another significant development that changed the landscape of New Haven by the beginning of the nineteenth century. On January 21, 1784, the state legislature passed an act to incorporate New Haven as a city. There is evidence to suggest that the town's freemen had wanted to become a city as early as December 9, 1771, or as the town records reveal:

> Whereas a motion was made to the town that this town might have the privileges of a city, and that proper measures might be taken to obtain the same, it is thereupon Vote that Roger Sherman [and seventeen others] be a Committee to take the same into consideration and judge of the motion what is best for the town to do with regard to the same and report thereupon to the town at another town-meeting.

There is no record of the committee's report thereafter and there is no other allusion to the charter until October 20, 1783, when the Connecticut state legislature was meeting in New Haven and President Stiles recorded in his diary, "Sign'd a petition to the Assembly for incorporating New Haven as a city." The petition, now preserved in the State Library in Hartford, contained 214 signatures and petitioned the state legislature for self-regulating powers as a city, for "it is a matter of no small importance that wharves, streets and highways, be commodious for business, and kept continually in good repair." In accordance with the petition a bill was passed by the Upper House, but the Lower House insisted on delaying the bill until the next session. In November,

A New Nation and the Road to Freedom

Stiles reported that they were now "Examining the Act or Charter proposed for the City of New Haven."

On January 5, three days before the next session of the General Assembly, the town of New Haven instructed its representatives Captain Henry Daggett and Captain Jesse Ford, "to exert themselves that the Act for incorporating a part of the town be passed with all convenient speed." They appear to have been successful, for on January 21 the Assembly granted New Haven its charter. "This afternoon," as Stiles recorded in his diary, "the Bill or Charter of the City of New Haven passed the Governor and Council, and completes the incorporation of the Mayor, four Aldermen, and twenty Common Council." The new government replaced the traditional town meeting. Besides the offices of a mayor, four aldermen, and twenty councilmen, a mayor's court was created to overlook civil cases within the city's jurisdiction while a number of other offices, like sheriff and treasurer, were created to better organize the city and regulate its commercial activities.

At the first election, which concluded on February 12, 1784, Roger Sherman, who was serving as a member of Congress in Annapolis, was elected mayor. He held the office until his death in 1793 (annual elections were introduced in 1826). Deacon Howell of the First Church, Deacon David Austin of the White Haven Church, Samuel Bishop from the town-clerk's office, and bookseller Isaac Beers were elected aldermen. Hezekiah Sabin was made treasurer, and Elias Stilwell and Parson Clark were the two sheriffs.

With the incorporation of New Haven, New London, Hartford, and Middletown asked the Connecticut legislature for their own city charters and received them. What is more, New Haven's borders narrowed to approximately their present shape, while Woodbridge, Hamden, North Haven, and East Haven became separate towns with their own charters. Soon there were municipal improvements, like the creation of a fire department (1788). The city purchased a fire engine and established a committee of six fire wardens to direct the volunteer firefighting force, composed of the male population between the ages of 16 and 60. The wardens were authorized to appoint four "sackmen" of good character, whose responsibility it was to attend fires and protect property in sacks after it had been removed.

Other municipal improvements were in the area of health. After Dr. Leverett Hubbard, New Haven's leading physician, had helped to found the County Medical Society (1784), the state legislature recognized the Connecticut Medical Society (1792), claiming that physicians "had become a truly professional group with standards to establish and maintain and professional leaning to exchange." The yellow fever and scarlet fever epidemics of 1794—together with a smallpox scare that same year—accentuated the issue of health in the city, which resulted in the creation of the Health Committee of the City of New Haven (1795), New Haven's first board of health.

In 1792 the state legislature chartered New Haven's first bank and, although the institution did not open its doors until 1796, David Austin became its first president. William Lyon was its first cashier. Two years later, it established the chamber of commerce in New Haven, one of the first in the United States, and its first meeting was held in the State House on the Green. Beautifying projects, such as the planting of elm trees and the preservation of older trees "for shade and ornamentation in this City," began in 1790 and earned New Haven the nickname "The City of Elms" after the Civil War. Samuel Woodworth, editor of *The Belles Lettres*, described Hillhouse's contribution during these years:

> Yon spacious "Green," the city boast and pride,
> Might still have been a barren commonwide,
> Had not a spirit worthy of the man,
> Conceived and urged to execute the plan,
> To screen it from a hackney'd long abuse,
> And consecrate it to a nobler use.

In 1796 James Hillhouse, together with Simeon Baldwin and others, established the Grove Street Cemetery and both men set out to improve the state's highways between 1797 and 1800 with the Hartford and New Haven Turnpike Company, founded for the purpose of constructing and repairing a highway between these two important centers. Both men were also the original members of the Connecticut Academy of Arts and Sciences, the third oldest learned society in the United States, which President Ezra Stiles had first conceived and which his successor Timothy Dwight affected in 1799. Dwight remarked in 1810 that it was the only literary society in New Haven and had contributed to the country by the publication of its *Transactions*.

If taxes had instigated the Revolutionary War, then New Haveners and state residents were paying more in taxes for these municipal departments and improvement projects. Even before then, at the close of the war, municipal taxes had doubled from their prewar level to 4 pence on the pound, or nearly 2¢ on the dollar, and state taxes had increased even more to 3 shillings and 2 pence on the pound, or 16¢ on the dollar. With a looming war debt, the state legislature, with New Haven's support, rejected Congress's requisition to levy import duties on specified articles without the approval of the state first. However, in the state election of 1784, New Haven and the rest of Connecticut gave its support for a stronger central government and granted Congress the right to levy a minimal federal tax.

This tension between state and federal rights eventually led to the Constitutional Convention of 1787 when delegates from the 13 states met at Philadelphia to amend the Articles of Confederation. During and after the Revolutionary War the United States had acted on and adhered to this first constitution, but with the Articles' emphasis on state rights, Congress became

A New Nation and the Road to Freedom

a limited and ineffective governing body for the early republic. Therefore, a convention of 55 delegates—including George Washington, Benjamin Franklin, James Madison, Alexander Hamilton, and Gouverneur Morris—met at Philadelphia in May of 1787 to amend the Articles, but the delegates went further. They drafted a completely new constitution, which resulted in the rise of Federalists and Anti-federalists and the first political party system of the United States, eventually culminating in a bloody civil war over pro-slavery/state rights and anti-slavery/federal rights.

The three Connecticut delegates to travel to Philadelphia were Oliver Ellsworth, William Samuel Johnson, and Roger Sherman. As the mayor of New Haven and representative to the first and second Continental Congresses, Sherman was a prolific statesman, the only founding father to sign all four revolutionary documents: the Articles of Association, the Articles of Confederation, the Declaration of Independence, and the Federal Constitution. At the Convention he played a key role, attending almost every session, sitting on the committee of Postponed Matters, and speaking no less than 138 times, but it was his and Oliver Ellsworth's introduction of the "Connecticut Compromise," otherwise known as the "Great Compromise," by which he made his greatest contribution to the constitutional history of the United States.

The "Connecticut Compromise" was simply a solution to the problem of representation that occurred at the Convention after James Madison and Edmund Randolph introduced the "Virginia Plan," a proposal calling for a bicameral legislature representing each of the states by the size of their population. Although this appealed to the larger states of Virginia, Pennsylvania, and Massachusetts, the smaller states of Georgia, Delaware, New Jersey, and New Hampshire opposed the idea and put forward William Paterson's "New Jersey Plan," which called for amendments to the Articles of Confederation while maintaining the Articles' unicameral legislature with one vote for each state. As the two factions argued, Roger Sherman and Oliver Ellsworth, who were associated with the middle-sized states of the Carolinas, Maryland, New York, and Connecticut, put forward a proposal first suggested by Benjamin Franklin, calling for a bicameral legislature with the lower house representing each of the states by population and the upper house representing each of the states on an equal footing. The Convention accepted the compromise, abandoning the unicameral legislature of the old constitution for a bicameral one. On January 9, 1788, the state of Connecticut ratified the Constitution by a vote of 128 to 40, becoming the fifth state to join the union and ushering in a new era of American history.

If "all men are created equal," as the founding fathers had declared in the Declaration of Independence, they did not reserve that right for women or African Americans. At the Convention, women were not given the franchise and there was an eerie silence regarding slavery, although many founding fathers, including Roger Sherman and Benjamin Franklin, opposed the institution on moral and economic grounds. This silence was no accident, as the founders knew that the issue would divide the states and destroy any hope of a union, as it almost would in the nineteenth century. But the issue was not going to fade away, as southern economies became more dependent on slave labor and the North became increasingly abolitionist. The contradictory view that all men were created equal while the institution of slavery continued in the United States can perhaps be explained by the language of the time, in which slaves were often referred to as commodities, as pieces of property, and not in the language of human lives. This economic interpretation became part of the pro-slavery rhetoric in the South during the nineteenth century and went so far as to argue for the protection of the slave owner's property under the federal Constitution.

But if this language explains one contradiction, it does not explain why the founding fathers included slaves as part of their state populations; in other words, why did they determine that each slave was the equivalent of three-fifths of a human life? As put forward in the "Connecticut Compromise," the population of each state would determine its representation in the lower congressional house, or the House of Representatives. In order to determine the population of each state, every five slaves were to be counted as three. This did not confer the vote on slaves; it was simply a way to determine representation as well as taxation, and in the final wording of the Constitution there was no mention of "slaves" or "slavery," simply "all other persons." But the meaning was clear enough: slaves were "persons" and sooner or later the contradiction would lead to a major conflict between the North and South. As Abraham Lincoln told a New Haven audience on March 6, 1860, a few months before his nomination to the presidency, "Slavery does not exist" in Connecticut and the North because "To us it appears natural to think that slaves are human beings: *men*, not property; that some of the things, at least, stated about men in the Declaration of Independence apply to them as well as to us."

More often than not we associate the history of slavery with the South, but New Haven—like a number of towns and cities in colonial America—was also an active participant in the slave trade. As a commercial seaport, it had participated in the slave trade from the very beginning and, unlike popular views of the North during the nineteenth century, did not completely wash its hands of the institution until the Emancipation Act of 1848. Some of the first slaves, including Indians, blacks, and whites, were likely indentured servants serving a term of bondage. However, by the end of the seventeenth century slavery had evolved into a hereditary and racial institution with blacks and Indians serving a life of bondage, although no slave law defined the institution as such. It simply existed, or as Governor Gurdon Saltonstall ruled in the 1704 appeal of a mulatto slave, Abda, whose father was English:

> According to the laws and constant practice of this Colony and all
> other plantations (as well as by the civil law) such persons as are

> born of negro bondwomen are themselves in like condition, i.e.
> born in servitude . . . and though the law of this Colony doth not say
> that such persons as are born of negro woman and supposed to be
> mulattoes shall be slaves (which was needless, because of the
> constant practice by which they are held as such), yet it saith
> expressly, that no man shall put away or make free his negro or
> mulatto slave, etc., which undeniably shows and declares an
> approbation of such servitude, and that mulattos may be held as
> slaves within this government.

Indian slavery proved to be problematic for the colonists, however, and the state legislature outlawed the Indian slave trade on July 8, 1715 after the importation of a number of Tuscarora slave warriors from South Carolina caused great alarm in Connecticut. According to the General Court, the Carolina Indians were a hostile people and had "committed many cruel and bloody outrages," and that "unless speedy care be taken" immediately, there was a "danger that greater numbers of them will be imported, whereby our Indians may be tempted to draw off to those enemies, and many other great mischiefs may ensue thereon." And so it ordered "that a prohibition shall be published against the importation of any Indian slaves whatsoever."

Such fears of a slave insurrection did not apply to African slavery; the institution survived the colonial period and grew in proportion to European trade with the West Indies and Africa. When the first settlers had come to New England some of them brought African slaves (or indentured servants) with them. Governor Theophilus Eaton and the Reverend John Davenport both owned slaves, though there is no evidence to suggest that Davenport's "One servant boy" was indeed a "negro." Eaton, however, "had two negro servants, bought with his money, servants forever or during his pleasure, according to Leviticus 25, 45, and 46." Their names were John and Lucretia Cram, and, according to the town records, Governor Eaton also owned "neagar Anthony." Edward Hopkins, the benefactor of the Hopkins Grammar School and the second governor of Connecticut Colony, was another first-generation slave owner; generations of Hopkins alumni have acknowledged him as a slave owner in the lines of their school song:

> Then he sailed away his fortune still to find.
> But he gave a colored gentleman and fourteen hundred pound,
> For to educate the folk he left behind.

The number of first-generation slave owners was small, however, and as the English Board of Trade reported in 1680, there were no more than 30 slaves in the colony.

Yet by the middle of the eighteenth century there had been a dramatic shift and the board now reported nearly 4,000 slaves living in the colony. At that time, it was also reported that there were 226 slaves in New Haven County: 106 in Branford, 59 in Guilford, 34 in Durham, 27 in Waterbury, and interestingly enough, none in New Haven, which was not the case as we shall see hereafter. By 1774, when Connecticut forbade the importation of slaves, there were 6,500 slaves in the colony, or about 3.4 percent of the entire population, the largest number of slaves in the colony at any given time. By 1790, after the Gradual Emancipation Act (1784), there were 2,648 slaves and 2,771 freed Africans; in 1800, there were nearly 1,000 slaves in Connecticut, about 80 of which, plus 130 freed Africans, lived in New Haven. This number continued to drop during the nineteenth century, with 310 in 1810, 97 in 1820, 25 in 1830, 17 in 1840, and 6 in 1848, when Connecticut abolished slavery completely.

That slavery was well planted in the New Haven area during the seventeenth and eighteenth centuries is evident from the colonial record. Ministers, who usually lived on farms and required farm hands, were likely to be slave owners. Among those owning slaves at the time were the Reverends Nicholas Street of East Haven; Samuel Whittlesey of Wallingford; Joseph Moss of Derby; Philemon Robbins of Branford; William Worthington of Saybrook; John Southmayd and John Leavenworth of Waterbury; David Humphreys of Seymour; Solomon Williams of Lebanon; Nathaniel Chauncey of Durham; Noadiah Russell of Middletown; Isaac Foster, Daniel Wadsworth, and Timothy Woodbridge of Hartford; Ebenezer Devotion of Suffield; Joseph Eliot of Guilford; Thomas Wells Bray of North Guilford; Jonathan Todd of East Guilford (now Madison); Jared Eliot of Killingworth (now Clinton); and John Davenport, Joseph Noyes, and Samuel Bird of New Haven. In their wills, Noyes left an estate of £3,600, including four African slaves; Whittlesey, who was also a trustee of Yale College, left an estate of £22,000, of which £1,400 were invested in "negro and molatto servants;" and Naphtali Daggett, Revolutionary War hero, president emeritus of Yale College, and professor of Divinity, left an estate in 1781 with about £100 invested in African slaves.

Other prominent slave owners at the time included Andrew and Marcus Baldwin of Woodbridge, Captain Titus Brockett of Wallingford, Captain Enos Atwater of Cheshire, and Juba Weston and Captains Daniel Holbrook and John Wooster of Seymour. In New Haven prominent names of slave owners included Joseph Tuttle, Isaac Jones, Benjamin Pardee, Stephen Munson, Elgin Goodrich, Jonathan Mansfield, Jared Ingersoll, Benjamin Isaacs, Samuel Mix, and John Townsend.

Despite the reality of slavery in Connecticut and New Haven, which was usually justified by Scripture and thereby part of God's natural order, it does not appear that the conditions of the institution were as harsh as the plantation system of the South. Law Professor Tapping Reeve once remarked:

> The master had no control over the life of his slave. If he killed him, he was liable to the same punishment as if he killed a freeman. A slave was capable of holding property in the character of devisee or legatee. If a slave married a free woman with the consent of his master, he was emancipated: for his master had suffered him to

contract a relation inconsistent with a state of slavery. The master by his consent had agreed to abandon his rights to him as a slave.

Besides a few protections under state law not available in the South, like the legal right of slaves to own property or sue their master in court, a closer relationship existed between master and slave in Connecticut than in the plantation system of the South, though admittedly the evidence is usually told from the master's point of view and we are left to wonder what the slave would have said if given half the chance. In what might be described as a concern for the spiritual welfare of the slave, Puritan masters took on a patriarchal role. In one example of this spiritual paternalism the soul of Hannah, the domestic servant of the Reverend Gershom Bulkley, was of paramount concern to her master; as Bulkley described it in his will:

> And in particular, to her my said [daughter] Dorothy Treat I give and bequeath my negro maid Hannah, willingly and solemnly requiring that in whose hands soever she may happen to come they use her well, and consider that she hath a soul to save as well as wee, and is a Christian; and therefore that they make conscience to promote her in her reading, catechism, and all Christianity, that she may profit and grow in religion and godliness and attain the end of baptism to the glory of God, and this I earnestly require on her behalf, as they will answer the neglect thereof before God.

A Mr. Meigs of East Guilford also showed the same concern for the spiritual condition of his slave Tom when their boat sprung a leak on the Sound. Having jumped in the water because the boat could hold only one person, Meigs explained his actions as a concern for Tom's spiritual state: "If I were drowned, I should go to heaven; but I don't think Tom would." This spiritual paternalism at times extended to the material world, such as when the Reverend Street's slave, also called Tom, used to ask his master periodically for his freedom, to which the reverend always responded regarding his obligations under the law: "You may be free any day, Tom, if you will let me draw up a writing that shall clear me from the obligation to take care of you when you are old and can earn nothing." Tom never took up the offer.

But some slaves demonstrated an openly dissident spirit to the institution, like Prince, a member of the Cornwall church, who refused to sit in the pew reserved for black clergy and was subsequently disciplined by the elders of the church. Mim, a slave of Ebenezer Marsh of Litchfield, did the same and shouted at several white youths that he would "strew the pew with the Gutts or Bowels of those who should dare to oppose his sitting in [the] pew." A fight ensued and other white congregationalists, witnessing the event, brought legal action against the youths. President Timothy Dwight of Yale College also recorded a story of dissent when he reported that a domestic servant in

Wallingford cut the throat of her master's daughter in the hope that she would receive her freedom and be sent back to Africa.

Such overt acts of defiance, however, were rare and relations between master and slave were generally good, though African Americans still found other ways to challenge the institution. As Sarah Kemble Knight of Boston noted in her journal, New Haveners are "too indulgent (especially the farmers) to their slaves, suffering too great familiarity from them, permitting them to sit at Table and eat with them, (as they say to save time,) and into the dish goes the black hoof as freely as the white hand." She also noted an incident involving a New Haven farmer:

> who had some difference with his slave, concerning something the master promised him and did not punctually perform; which caused some harsh words between them; But at length they put the matter to Arbitration and Bound themselves to stand to the award of such as they named—which done, the Arbitrators Having heard the Allegations of both parties, Order the master to pay 40 shillings to black face, and acknowledge his fault, And so the matter ended; the poor master very honestly standing to the award.

African Americans also asserted themselves during the Revolutionary War. In Connecticut, they had served in small numbers alongside whites in the militia, but were excluded from service when George Washington made the decision after the battles of Lexington and Concord to "reject negroes" from the army. The decision was reversed by the end of 1777 and Connecticut actively recruited African Americans, both slaves and freedmen. The historian David O. White has indentified over 300 African-American military men in Connecticut, many of whom served in white regiments at first, but formed an all-black company attached to the Fourth Connecticut Regiment in 1781, commanded by Colonel Zebulon Butler. (David Humphreys was the nominal commander as he was serving as Washington's aide-de-camp after the formation of the regiment.) The company was comprised of white officers and black privates. According to the payroll book of the Second Company, located at the New Haven Colony Historical Society (Fourth Regiment Paybook), black and white privates appear to have received the same provisions, discipline, and pay, indicating that the army provided a sense a equality among black and white regulars.

Freedom was one of the main enticements for slaves to join the Patriot cause. Bristol Baker of New Haven, who served in three regiments before his discharge in 1783, received his emancipation the following year, his master thinking it reasonable that he should be set free as he has been fighting for the "Liberties of the Country." Chatman Freeman, a slave of Noah Yale of Wallingford, was also granted his freedom after serving in place of his master's son, but Jack Arabas, who was serving in place of his master's 18-year-old son, returned home to the betrayal of his master. Apparently Captain Thomas Ivers of Newfield (now part of Bridgeport) changed his mind and wanted his former slave to remain in bondage. Arabus fled to New Haven and was arrested, but soon received his freedom after Judge James Wadsworth ruled in favor of manumission.

When the British invaded New Haven in 1779, at least two African Americans, "Pompey and another negro," were among the fatalities, the former having died defending the town. Before the British withdrawal, General Garth ordered a proclamation to be read on Long Wharf promising freedom to any slaves who left with the British fleet. There is no evidence that any African-American slaves left with the British, but we do know that Tory slaves—like those belonging to Thomas Darling—received their freedom. One slave whom we know did not leave with the British fleet was Lantz (or Lant), an African slave belonging to the Townsend family. When the British forces were withdrawing, a group of soldiers insisted that Lantz carry their booty. The son of John Townsend quickly intervened and carried the plunder himself, perhaps suspecting that the family would lose Lantz to the British.

In the last quarter of the eighteenth century, residents in New Haven and the surrounding towns were increasingly opposed to the institution of slavery. Rachel Johnson of Wallingford freed her slaves in 1778, saying that the main reason was "Because I Believe that all Mankind ought to be free." When Thomas Hooker of Farmington went to fight at Lexington in 1775, he freed his slave with the words, "I will not fight for liberty and leave a slave at home." Ebenezer Johnson of Derby emancipated his slave Roger so that he could "deal and act for himself." After the war, leading citizens also took an active role in the anti-slavery movement. Simeon Jocelyn and his brother Nathaniel (the painter who later captured the likeness of Cinqué in a painting now hanging in the New Haven Colony Historical Society) spoke out against the institution, as did Theodore Dwight, Theodore Dwight Woolsey, and the Reverend Leonard Bacon.

Although many of the clergy were slave owners in New Haven and other towns in Connecticut, they emerged in the last quarter of the eighteenth century as leading abolitionists. A number of religious pamphlets and sermons spoke of the evils of slavery, and between 1773 and 1774, the Reverends Ebenezer Baldwin and Jonathan Edwards Jr. published a series of articles on the sinfulness of slavery in the New Haven *Connecticut Journal.* Edwards, in a sermon on "The Impolicy and Injustice of the Slave Trade and Slavery," later compared the injustices of slavery with the late Revolutionary War: "Great Britain in her late attempt to enslave America, committed a very small crime indeed in comparison with the crime of those who enslave Africans."

Unlike his well-known father, who had owned slaves and even condoned the institution in his writings, Edwards confronted the issue of slavery head on and exposed the injustices of the institution at the national level. The Reverend Jonathan Todd of Guilford also came to the conclusion that slavery was unjust; in his will of 1791 he freed his slaves, adding, "I have long been convinced in my own mind that the enslaving of Africans brought from Africa or those born in this country is unjust; and that it is one of the sins of the land, and I would endeavor to free my estate from the cry of such a sin against it."

Another abolitionist who was also part of the ministerial class was the perennial Ezra Stiles. As a young minister in Newport, Rhode Island, Stiles bought a slave from Africa for a hogshead of whiskey and named him Newport. Newport was baptized and admitted as a full member of the Newport church (without voting privileges) and was freed when Stiles came to New Haven. He followed his former master to New Haven with a wife and child and was employed by Stiles for seven years at £20 per annum. Before he died in 1827 at the good old age of 90, Stiles's daughter provided for him, or as one Yale student remarked in 1818, Newport "is well and provided with a goose and turkey for Thanksgiving."

In August of 1790, Stiles and Simeon Baldwin founded the Connecticut Society for the Promotion of Freedom and for the Relief of Persons Unlawfully Holden to Bondage, which was later shortened to The African Society. Stiles became the first president and Baldwin the first secretary. The society met at both Hartford and New Haven each year and promoted the abolition of slavery, but it did not go so far as to promote the immediate abolition of slavery or deny the legal right of citizens to own slaves. Instead it took a practical approach, as declared in the agreement of the association:

> Impressed with a sense of the inestimable worth and value of the excellent constitution, laws, and government of this State and the United States of America, and anxiously desirous that every description of men who have obtained a residence among us, of whatever clime or colour, should quietly enjoy the freedom and happiness which the beneficent father of the human race has kindly allotted to us, and having with grief and abhorrence long beheld a considerable number of our fellow men groaning under the iron hand of Slavery, many of whom are entitled by the wise and humane laws of our country to an exemption from this cruel bondage; and being desirous to cooperate in a systematic way with the several societies which have been or that may be hereafter formed in the united States or elsewhere for the purpose of promoting the abolition of Slavery. . . .

By 1794, the society was taking the issue of abolishing slavery to the national level and began to attend conventions with other abolitionist societies in New York, Pennsylvania, New Jersey, and even in the slave states of Delaware, Maryland, and Virginia.

The abolition of slavery in New Haven and Connecticut, however, was the result of a series of laws passed over 75 years, beginning with a law in 1774 in which the Connecticut legislature forbade the importation of slaves, not because of any concern for the welfare of "negroes," but because it was thought "the increase of slaves in this Colony is injurious to the Poor and inconvenient." Economic conditions, namely competition between the laboring classes, contributed to the first anti-slavery law in Connecticut and "will perhaps go farther," as the father of American English and lexicography Noah Webster pointed out, "in abolishing the practice . . . than any declaration on the immorality and cruelty of the practice" *(see illustration on page 76).* The clergy and religious organizations, however, spoke increasingly of the immorality and wickedness of the institution and became the leading spokesmen and women of the abolition movement in the nineteenth century. By the end of 1783 President Stiles, noting the large number of African slaves brought into the United States in recent years, spoke not in the language of economics, but in that of human lives: "The constant annual importation of negroes into America and the West Indies is supposed to have been of late years about 60,000. Is it possible to think of this without horror?"

The following year, the legislature passed the Gradual Emancipation Act, stipulating that no child born into slavery would be a slave after the age of 25 (amended to 21 in 1797), but the slave trade and institution persisted despite a decrease in the overall number of slaves in both New Haven and Connecticut. John Sedgwick, as one example, bought a three-year-old African girl after the passage of the act and answered his critics by saying that the purchase was legal and that she would receive the same freedom as his children when she was of age. The continuation of slavery was not lost on the slave population itself, and in 1788 the Blacks of New Haven City petitioned the state legislature asking for their freedom. Firstly, because "we are Drag[ge]d from our native Country for Life lyis Cruil Slavirre Le[a]ving our mothers our farthers our Sisters and our Brothers is this humen pea[p]le." Secondly, because

> after we have Be[e]n and fought the grandest Battles that has Be[e]n fought in this War the greats part of us, We and our children and our Brothers ar[e] takend By fo[r]se of vialince and carr[i]ed whear thay Suffer an Addisan[a]l Sufrans wher[e] we ar[e] Beaten and whealmed with Out Eni Cries or with eni Law Gentlemen[.] Will is this to Be Rite and justes[?] Is this a free co[u]ntry[?] No it [is] murder.

Thirdly, because

> you will freely allow us a human Bodys . . . as a pr[e]ss[h]us Sole to Save and how shal we and how shall we Ever obtain that en[d] rest in Jesus Christ for the Lov[e] of our pressh[es] Soles[?] When ar[e] we to seek it when wee ar[e] a gr[eat me[ny] of us reprived of going to the house Gods to attend pubblick woship or much more l[e]arning us our C A B or to reed the holy BiBle So as to [k]no[w] the word of god[?]

Fourthly, because

> we wo[u]ld wish to act a wisely part and with a mil[d]e Temper and good Dispersisan but can we help but Beg for murcy in this accation[.] Don[t] gentlemen think us impirtinent for asking this favor for the Lord [h]ath saide ask and it Shal [be] given[.] We that can live pray let you us Liv[e].

And fifthly, because

> all our wishes ar[e] that your Honours wou[ld] grant us a Liberration[.] We are all Deturmand we Can to[il.] As Long as th[e]ir is Labor we woul[d] wish no more to be in Sl[avery] to Sin See[i]n[g]e Christ is maid us free and na[i]l[e]d our tanants to the Cross and Bought our Liberty.

African Americans still sought their freedom, and as the number of freed slaves increased at the end of the eighteenth century with the Gradual Emancipation Act, one still found the occasional advertisement in the newspapers of an individual or family of "negroes" for sale, to whom "a good title will be given." In the *New Haven Gazette* of November 9, 1786, there was the following advertisement: "To be sold at public Vendue on Tuesday the 29th of November, instant, at the dwelling house of Capt. Enos Atwater of Cheshire, deceased, a good Negro Wench, about twenty years old." And for April 19, 1787, in the same newspaper there was "To be sold, a healthy, strong and active Negro Boy, about 11 years of age." The slave trade persisted, as one Connecticut slave recounted after the Civil War, "slaves were driven through the streets tied or fastened together for market. This seems to surprise some that I meet, but it was true. I have it from reliable authority. Yes, this was done in Connecticut."

In New Haven County, which had maintained a small slave population in relation to other counties in the state during the colonial period, the slave population had declined to about 500 by 1800, but this was still twice the number of any other county in the state. New Haveners, however, were now confronting the institution head on and organizing emancipation and African improvement societies. Like Ezra Stiles and Simeon Baldwin, who had founded the first Connecticut anti-slavery society, other New Haveners looked to the plight of African Americans and took municipal action. In 1811, New Haven founded the Artisan Street School, the first school in the city to instruct "colored students." Another segregated school was founded in 1825, but the condition of these schools was poor at best and New Haven's African-American population received no more than primary education during the first half of the eighteenth century. A year earlier, the city had formally recognized the United African Society, organized by Simeon Jocelyn in 1820, which became New Haven's first independent African-American congregation. The church was located on Temple Street and was later relocated to Dixwell Avenue, where it became the Dixwell United Church of Christ. James Pennington, an escaped slave, served as its first minister and was succeeded by Amos Gerry Beman, a passionate African-American abolitionist. Improvement societies for African Americans soon followed, with the founding of the African Improvement Society of New Haven (1826) and the New Haven Anti-Slavery Society (1833), one of the first societies for the immediate and complete abolition of slavery.

While New Haven moved gradually towards emancipation after the War of Independence, the *Amistad* incident of 1839 put the city at the center of the national slavery debate and soon brought a complete end to slavery in Connecticut. The incident occurred when 53 Mendi Africans were abducted from the coast of Sierra Leone and shipped to Havana, Cuba, where two Spanish planters—Don José Ruiz and Don Pedro Montez—purchased them for $450 apiece and placed them aboard the schooner *La Amistad* for Guanaja, a sugar plantation on the other side of the island. The vessel set sail on August 28 and, three days later, the Mendians mutinied under the leadership of Sengbe Pieh (Joseph Cinqué), killing the captain and cook. After setting the crew adrift in a small boat, they ordered Ruiz and Montez to sail the *Amistad* to Africa; however, knowing nothing of navigation, they did not notice that the Spanish planters were changing the course of the schooner at night to a northwest direction, and after almost two months at sea they were seized by the U.S. brig *Washington* off the coast of Long Island, New York. The planters were released and the Mendians placed in the New Haven County Jail on charges of murder and piracy, which were eventually dropped. But the question of property rights still loomed, as the Spanish planters attempted to reclaim their property and Lieutenants Richard W. Meade and Thomas R. Gedney of the USS *Washington* made salvage claims on the *Amistad* and its cargo.

Although U.S. President Martin Van Buren supported the planters' property claims, abolitionists in the North, including Lewis and Arthur Tappan, Simeon and Nathaniel Jocelyn, and Samuel Dutton, opposed any such action and raised funds for the Africans' defense. They retained Roger Sherman Baldwin of New Haven as the chief defense counsel, who, together with Seth P. Staples and Theodore Sedgwick Jr., defended the Mendians against the property claims of Ruiz and Montez and the Spanish government, as well as the salvage claims of Meade and Gedney. The case was moved from the United States Circuit Court to the United States District Court in New Haven. On January 8, Judge Andrew T. Judson ruled that Meade and Gedney were entitled to one-third of the value of the *Amistad* and its cargo, but that such property did not include the Mendians, as they had no value as property under Connecticut law. Moreover, he ruled that the Africans had been captured in violation of Spanish law and that they were neither slaves nor Spanish subjects and were therefore free by "the law of Spain itself."

Judson's ruling had both political and legal ramifications. An appeal was brought before the Circuit Court, which upheld the District Court's decision, but because the case had become a major issue between the United States and Spain, Judge Thompson ruled that the case should go before the Federal Supreme Court the following January. The defense, knowing that they needed an attorney of national renown to present the case before the justices of the Supreme Court (five of whom were from the South), approached John Quincy Adams, who had given counsel during the New Haven trial, and persuaded the former President to take on the case. On February 20, 1841, the case opened and Baldwin spoke for the defense. Four days later Adams made his argument, demonstrating that the executive office had breached its constitutional powers by negotiating with the Spanish to remove the Mendians after the first trial; in other words, President Van Buren, expecting the defense to lose, had a vessel waiting in the New Haven harbor to transfer the Mendians to the Spanish before the defense had a chance to launch an appeal. He also demonstrated that the *Antelope* case, in which the United States returned African slaves to the Spanish, had no bearing on the *Amistad* case, as the Spanish law against the foreign slave trade had not taken effect at that time, and the Mendians, having been captured illegally, had a right to mutiny and claim their freedom. Although Adams's argument against the executive branch had no effect on the final decision of the Supreme Court, the justices ruled in favor of the Mendians, who were "entitled to their freedom . . . to be free . . . and go without delay." On November 27 the Medians returned to Africa, where 35 of their original number resettled, the rest having died either awaiting trial or on the voyage home *(see illustration on page 77)*.

The *Amistad* trial enraged the pro-slavery interests in the South, but abolition sentiment in the North—especially in New Haven and Connecticut—had grown significantly in the late 1830s and early 1840s. By 1844 the state legislature had ruled that no judge, justice of the peace, or any other officer was allowed to issue a warrant "for the arrest or detention of any person escaping into this State; claimed to be fugitive from labor or service as a slave," or grant a certificate to their claimants. It was only a matter of time before New Haven and Connecticut abolished slavery completely, which occurred in the year 1848 when the state legislature ruled "that no person shall hereafter be held in slavery in this State," that emancipated slaves must be supported by their masters, and that no slave shall be brought into Connecticut. Yet by this point, slavery had all but disappeared in the state through the gradual process of manumission. So when the legislature passed its resolution Connecticut had no more than six slaves, all over the age of 64, making the clause regarding the support of former slaves all but irrelevant.

The resolution made all African Americans free in the state of Connecticut, but freedom did not bring equality. African Americans faced racism in their daily lives and were denied the vote. Many lived in squalid conditions in a slum near the mouth of Mill River and were treated unfairly by their fellow citizens. They were prohibited from serving as apprentices and many worked in the homes of the wealthy and middle class. Others worked as barbers, hotel waiters, and tailors, but menial labor was their lot. Emancipation did not bring social and economic advancement, and without the franchise, they were left to create their own political and social traditions. As New Haven's historian Rollin G. Osterweis described their political and social attempts at inclusion, they

> lived a life so completely separated from the rest of the community that they were obliged to develop their own social and political customs. Barred from the franchise, they developed colorful imitations of the regular election proceedings, staging parades, speeches, and lavish entertainment in connection with choosing "African Governors" who were accorded a certain amount of unofficial power and prestige among them.

The "Black Governors," who served as mediators between the black community and white establishment, were not always elected but wielded a certain amount of power and prestige in their own communities. Some even had assistants and sheriffs, but they also served the interest of the white establishment, like handing out severe punishments to slaves who had violated the law. This probably made them unpopular in their communities too. Hartford, Norwich, Seymour, Derby, and other towns in Connecticut all elected or appointed black governors. So did New Haven, for as far as we know, William Lanson, Quash Piere, and Thomas Johnson served as black governors from approximately 1825 to 1837.

Although a number of white New Haveners had advocated the abolition of slavery during the late eighteenth and early nineteenth centuries, they often did not want freed African Americans living in New Haven or next to them. As the historian Howard Jones has noted, the people of Connecticut opposed slavery and "did not favor its spread into western territories," but "this did not mean that they welcomed blacks." New Haveners were no different and even the Reverend Leonard Bacon, Jehudi Ashmun, Charles A. Ingersoll, and Roger Sherman—all prominent New Haven abolitionists—were advocates of sending freed slaves back to Africa. Organized in 1818, the American Society for Colonizing the Free People of Colour of the United States, later called the American Colonization Society, had followers in New Haven, who the following year organized the New Haven Auxiliary Colonizing Society to cooperate with the mother society. The Colonization Society attracted a number of prominent Americans, including Abraham Lincoln, and as a means of ameliorating conditions for freed blacks as well as relieving white fears of a large black population in the South, it promoted the idea of return migration. Some African Americans supported the society's goals but in 1827, the country's first African-American newspaper, *Freedom's Journal*, began to circulate under the editorship of Samuel Cornish and responded to this notion of African colonization with the following solemn declaration:

New Haven

We are content to remain where we are. We do not believe that things will always continue the same. The time must come when the declaration of independence will be felt in the heart as well as muttered from the mouth, and when the rights of all shall be properly acknowledged and appreciated. . . . This is our home and our country. Beneath its sod lies the bones of our fathers: for it, some of them fought, bled, and died. Here we were born and here we will die.

And so racism persisted in New Haven and the United States as immediate abolitionists attacked the institution itself. Consequently, it was no surprise that a number of New Haveners opposed and responded violently to the proposal put forward by Simeon Jocelyn at the African-American Convention in Philadelphia (1831), that New Haven—with all its beauty, piety, intellect, friendliness, humanity, and generosity—would be the ideal location for a "Negro college." The public greeted the proposal with outrage; newspapers condemned it, and the mayor, aldermen, councilmen, and freemen of the city called an emergency meeting and passed a series of resolutions against the proposal and against the abolition movement itself. Assaults against African Americans took place in the streets of New Haven and climaxed in September when "the best citizens in New Haven, led by the mayor and a number of Yale professors and students staged a riot before the homes of supporters of the college." A few weeks later, another mob descended on an African-American neighborhood, nicknamed "New Liberia," and assaulted 14 white men and four white women for befriending and socializing with African Americans.

Three years later Jocelyn was forced to quit officiating at the African church, and in 1837 a mob laid siege to his residence. Evidently Jocelyn's views were not popular. At a city meeting on September 9, 1835, the citizens of New Haven voted to stop the abolitionists' "transmission of incendiary information" through the mail, to support the colonization of "the free colored population" back to Africa, and "viewed with alarm the efforts of the Abolitionists." Such actions obviously were part of an attempt at reconciliation with the South, but even then there were evident signs of racism as mob violence permeated the streets of New Haven.

After the "gag rule" of 1836 and 1837, and the *Amistad* incident of 1839, sentiment towards the South changed rapidly and, as the Civil War drew closer, New Haven sided increasingly with the abolitionists. In 1848 it became illegal to own slaves in New Haven. The abolition of slavery did not occur in the South until after the Civil War, but in both the North and South, the specter of racism persisted in its many forms and shapes, and persists to this day in its various disguises.

Chapter Four

THE CIVIL WAR AND
THE ROAD TO PROSPERITY

On April 15, 1861, three days after the South attacked Fort Sumter, President Abraham Lincoln issued a call for 75,000 Connecticut volunteers to serve for a term of three months. Governor William Buckingham answered the call by forming two Connecticut regiments, the second one being based in New Haven under the command of Colonel Alfred Howe Terry. The New Haven Grays voted unanimously to join the war effort and formed Company A of the Second Regiment of Connecticut Infantry. At the same time two Irish companies—the Emmett Guards and the McGowan Guards—volunteered their services and joined the Second Regiment.

After the Battle of Bull Run, it was clear that the war would last more than three months and Connecticut restructured its infantry, creating nine regiments. Colonel John L. Chatfield took command of the Sixth Regiment and Colonel Terry the Seventh, while Colonel Thomas W. Calhill took command of the largely Irish-born Ninth. As the war continued, Governor Buckingham called for more regiments and offered "soldier's bounties" of $80 to $200 depending on the size of a recruit's family. The federal government also offered bounties of $250 and, in August 1862, New Haven offered its own bounties of $100. Thomas R. Trowbridge together with other citizens of New Haven raised funds for private bounties, but as the war dragged on and volunteers were increasingly less forthcoming, the federal government was forced to pass the National Draft Act, introducing conscription in the North.

Among the first volunteers of the Connecticut regiments was an obscure New Havener named Frederick R. Jackson. At 17 years of age, and just two days after passing his Yale College entrance exams, he joined Company F of the Seventh Regiment and, as first sergeant, marched south in October 1861. By the following spring he had fought at Port Royal, South Carolina, and at Fort Pulaski, Georgia. That summer he fought at the battle of James Island (in Charleston, South Carolina) where fellow New Havener Captain Edwin S. Hitchcock fell, and where he led a daybreak charge on Fort Lamar. During the assault a canister from a cannon hit Jackson in the left arm above the elbow, shattering the limb, but still he kept charging. According to *Military Order, Congress Medal of Honor Legion of the United States* (1905):

> He grasped the shattered and bloody stump and went on in command of his company during the charge and during two of the subsequent charges, until he finally fell powerless through unavoidable loss of blood, though he had grasped and squeezed the bleeding stump as hard as he could, to prevent his bleeding to death.

Jackson lay unconscious on the field for over 17 hours and was then taken prisoner by the Confederate Army. A surgeon amputated his arm without chloroform and, after four months as a prisoner of war, he returned to New Haven where, "Upon my return my friends supposed me dead and my mother was dressed in mourning for me."

Jackson was not ready to retire from military service, however; within months he was in Washington, where he took command of the newly formed Invalid Corps, later called the Veteran Reserve Corps. There he met President Lincoln, with whom he conversed on a regular basis, and it was Lincoln who "picked me out to command the guard of honor" when he went to Gettysburg to dedicate the national cemetery. This much was true, but Jackson no doubt fabricated—or exaggerated—the rest of the account when he said, "It was well that the great war president had a guard on that occasion, for an attempt was made in Baltimore by a gang of roughs to get into his car."

As President Lincoln and Secretary of War Edwin Stanton traveled through the streets in their horse-driven car, a crowd apparently climbed up onto the platform of the car. "We tried to get the fellows off the platform," Jackson told the New Haven *Register*, "but they persisted and packed on like sardines. I at last ordered my men to use the bayonet and we pricked several of them before they would jump down. Secretary Stanton always claimed that those fellows were bent on assassinating the president and that only my guard saved him."

As Lincoln's unofficial bodyguard, Jackson spent a lot of time with the President and had access to the private life of the first family. Young "Tad" was the "pet" of the family, said Jackson, and had a knack for causing mischief. In one instance, when Jackson was showing the White House to a group of friends from Connecticut, young Tad told them they would have to pay $1 to see the President's house. "There were 18 of us," recalled Jackson, "and each one forked over $1. After he had shown us around what do you think Tad did? Why, he went out and met an Italian peanut vendor whose stand was nearby, bought the outfit, had it moved over near the White House grounds and began selling peanuts. When the president found out about his boy's practical joke he was so mortified and angry that he almost cried."

Jackson saw action again when Lincoln sent him to take command of Fort Kearney and hold off General Jubal Early's advance. He held the fort for five days, long enough for reinforcements to arrive. When he heard of Lincoln's assassination in April 1865, he was on leave in New Haven but "took the first train for Washington and upon my arrival, Mr. Stanton assigned me to the charge of forming the escort of officers who were to march in the procession." The following month he resigned his commission and left the military for good, retiring to New Haven where he was sometimes seen wearing the Congressional Medal of Honor pinned to his coat, which he was awarded after the battle of James Island.

Two of New Haven's most notable officers during the Civil War were Alfred Howe Terry and Andrew Hull Foote. The former, a clerk of New Haven

Continued on page 101

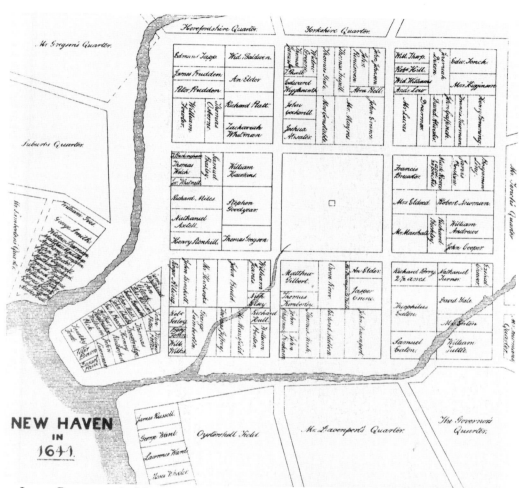

JOHN BROCKETT'S MAP OF 1641. *There has been considerable speculation about the architect of the original town plan (i.e. Lion Gardiner, Robert Seeley, and John Brockett) without any conclusive evidence. Brockett's map, however, is the oldest surviving map of the New Haven Colony, listing the names and home lots of the original investors who occupied the eight squares surrounding the "market place" and the two suburban sections extending to the waterfront (then much closer to the town center than it is today). (NHCHS)*

HENRY WHITEFIELD'S STONE HOUSE. *Built in 1639, the structure is the oldest house in Connecticut and the oldest stone house in New England. It appears on the National Register of Historic Places and is now the Henry Whitfield State Museum in Guilford, Connecticut (modern spelling has removed the first "e" from Whitefield's name).*

JESSE TALBOT'S PAINTING (C. 1850) OF THE PHANTOM SHIP AS IT APPEARED IN NEW HAVEN IN JUNE 1647. *New Haven settlers and two gentlemen in the foreground (possibly Governor Theophilus Eaton and the Reverend John Davenport) observe the apparition in the distance. (NHCHS)*

CENTER CHURCH ON THE GREEN. *A few yards back from the site of the first meetinghouse, which also served as the First Church of New Haven, it was built by Ithiel Town between 1812 and 1815 and its interior was remodeled by Henry Austin in 1842. In the old burying-gound behind the church Colonel John Dixwell, one of the three regicides; and Theophilus Eaton, the first governor of the colony, are buried. (NHFPL) On their monuments are these inscriptions:*

J.D. ESQ. DECEASED MARCH Y^E 18TH. IN Y^E 82^{D.} YEAR OF HIS AGE. 1688–9.

THEOPHILUS EATON FIRST GOVERNOR OF THE NEW HAVEN COLONY.
Eaton so faimed so wise so just. The Phoenix of our world here hides his dust.
The name forget, N. England never must.

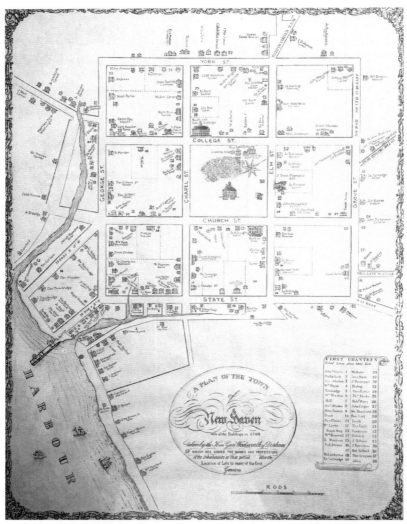

"A PLAN OF THE TOWN OF NEW HAVEN" BY JAMES WADSWORTH FOR THE YEAR 1748. The map illustrates the growing prosperity of New Haven in the first half of the eighteenth century and identifies John Dixwell's house on the corner of Grove and College Streets. (YUL)

JONATHAN EDWARDS (1703–1758), YALE GRADUATE AND MINISTER OF NORTHAMPTON, MASS. Edwards was a prominent supporter of the religious revivals spreading throughout New England and the rest of the colonies during the 1730s and 1740s. (Benson J. Lossing's Lives of Celebrated Americans*)*

JONATHAN TRUMBULL (1710–1785). Trumbull was born in Lebanon, Connecticut, and was elected lieutenant governor of Connecticut in 1766. He also served as governor of the colony and state from 1769 to 1784. (Benson J. Lossing's The Pictorial Field-Book of the Revolution*)*

DAVID WOOSTER (1711–1777). A Yale graduate and veteran commander of the French and Indian War, Wooster became a major general in the Connecticut miltia. He fell mortally wounded while defending the town of Danbury, Connecticut, against a British invasion in 1777. (Benson J. Lossing's The Pictorial Field-Book of the Revolution)

CAPTAIN JOSEPH WADSWORTH HIDING THE ORIGINAL CHARTER IN THE WYLLYS ESTATE OAK TREE. In Benson J. Lossing, Our Country: A Household History for All Readers, from the discovery of America to the One Hundredth Anniversary of the Declaration of Independence.

SAVIN'S ROCK. This is where General Garth and his troops landed during the British invasion on July 5, 1779. (Benson J. Lossing's The Pictorial Field-Book of the Revolution)

SAVIN'S ROCK.

BENEDICT ARNOLD (1741-–1801), NEW HAVEN RESIDENT AND REVOLUTIONARY WAR HERO. Arnold later betrayed the American revolutionary cause and lived the remainder of his days as an exile in England. In Benson J. Lossing, Our Country: A Household History for All Readers, from the Discovery of America to the One Hundredth Anniversary of the Declaration of Independence.

WEST BRIDGE AND MILFORD HILL. This site is where the American militia encountered British troops during the invasion of New Haven on July 5, 1779. (Benson J. Lossing's The Pictorial Field-Book of the Revolution*)*

WOOD ENGRAVING OF JOHN W. BARBER'S MONUMENT TO ADJUTANT WILLIAM CAMPBELL. It was close to the place where Campbell fell mortally wounded during the British invasion of New Haven and was destroyed by vandals in 1872. (Benson J. Lossing's The Pictorial Field-Book of the Revolution*)*

VIEW OF NEW HAVEN FROM THE SOUTH, 1800. The city was growing and prospering as a commercial seaport town and soon became one of the nation's manufacturing capitals. (NHFPL)

SAMUEL F.B. MORSE'S PAINTING (C. 1822) OF ELI WHITNEY (1765–1825). Whitney invented the cotton gin and was a New Haven gun manufacturer. (NHCHS)

Judges' Cave on the summit of West Rock. Where Edward Whalley and William Goffe hid from the king's officials. (NHFPL)

BEERS'S TAVERN ON THE CORNER OF CHAPEL AND COLLEGE STREETS. Where Benedict Arnold ordered Lieutenant Leavenworth to demand the powder-house keys from the selectmen of the town. George Washington also spent the night at the tavern when he passed through New Haven on July 2, 1775, on his way to take command of the Continental Army in Boston. (NHFPL)

HENRY AUSTIN'S WATERCOLOR (1848) OF NEW HAVEN'S FIRST RAILROAD STATION AT THE CORNER OF CHAPEL AND UNION STREETS. (YUL)

NOAH WEBSTER'S MONUMENT IN THE GROVE STREET CEMETERY. *Webster was born in a western division of Hartford (later West Hartford), Connecticut, but spent most of his adult life in New Haven, where he worked on simplifying the English language and compiling the first American dictionary, which contained over 70,000 entries when it was completed in 1828. Webster died on May 28, 1843, in New Haven.*

YALE COLLEGE'S CONNECTICUT HALL AND CHAPEL (ATHENAEUM), 1786. *Both structures, situated behind the old hall, facing the Green (which the college removed in 1782), were built in the Georgian style during the early 1750s and 1760s. They were also the first brick buildings in New Haven, predating the brick meetinghouse on the Green. (NHFPL)*

Statue of Abraham Pierson on the Old Yale Campus. Pierson founded Branford and helped found Newark. He was also Yale's first rector.

Sengbe Pieh (Joseph Cinqué). This bronze statue portrays the leader of the Amistad slave revolt, located in front of City Hall on the exact site where the mutineers were held in the County Jail.

UNION SOLDIERS ON THE NEW HAVEN GREEN, 1864. *New Haven's support for the northern cause was divided until the closing months of the war. In the presidential election of 1860, for example, the number of combined Democratic votes for John C. Breckenridge and Stephen A. Douglas were nearly equal to those of Lincoln (a vote of 3,012 to 3,140), and when General George B. McClellan, the Democrat candidate who advocated appeasement with the South, visited New Haven on the eve of the 1864 presidential election, residents turned up by the thousands to cheer for him. McClellan lost the election by a close margin, and it was only the Union successes in Virginia, together with the eventual assassination of Lincoln the following year, that the city became overwhelmingly loyal to the northern cause. (YUL)*

CONNECTICUT STATEHOUSE ON THE NEW HAVEN GREEN. Built in 1828 by Ithiel Town in the Greek Revival style and demolished in 1889, after New Haven ceased to be the state co-capital with Hartford. (NHFPL)

DEMOLITION OF THE CONNECTICUT STATEHOUSE ON THE NEW HAVEN GREEN, 1889. Despite the protests of many residents, city officials levelled the structure, destroying an important landmark and part of the city's heritage. (YUL)

GRAND AVENUE, FAIR HAVEN. *This area is where a number of Irish immigrants settled during the nineteenth century. (NHFPL)*

ST. MARY'S CHURCH ON HILLHOUSE AVENUE. *Built by James Murphy in one of the more patrician and Protestant areas of New Haven, the 1870 structure and its location represent the growing wealth and influence of the Irish community. (NHFPL)*

CHAPEL STREET LOOKING EAST AT THE CORNER OF COLLEGE STREET WITH A BICYCLE IN THE FOREGROUND. *(NHFPL)*

ELM STREET BETWEEN TEMPLE AND CHURCH STREETS. *Bristol house is in the foreground,* c. 1900. *(NHFPL)*

ENTRANCE GATE TO THE GROVE STREET CEMETERY. *Designed in 1845 by the architect Henry Austin, it is a solid brown stone structure with two colonnades and the inscription,* "THE DEAD SHALL BE RAISED." *(NHFPL)*

ENTRANCE TO HAMILTON PARK ON WHALLEY AVENUE DURING THE 1870s. *The park, orginally called Brewster Park, was one of New Haven's first planned parks. (YUL)*

STUDENTS SITTING ON THE OLD YALE FENCE AT THE CORNER OF CHAPEL AND COLLEGE STREETS, 1886–1888. The fence, which has since been removed, marked the division between Town and Gown. (YUL)

Stanley Street Entrance, Edgewood Park. Donald Grant Mitchell developed the park after buying a 360-acre farm in Westville and turning it into public park in 1889. (NHFPL)

RAILROAD TRACK IN CUSTOM HOUSE SQUARE ON THE CORNER OF STATE AND WATER STREETS. (NHFPL)

VIEW FROM GROVE AND YORK STREETS OF THE STERLING LAW BUILDINGS UNDER CONSTRUCTION, JULY 7, 1930. With the generous bequests of John William Sterling and Edward S. Harkness, Yale University commenced a massive building project during the 1920s and 1930s, which included ten residential colleges, professional and graduate schools, a new gymnasium, and the Sterling Memorial Library. (YUL)

THE CONSTRUCTION SITE OF THE NEW HAVEN FREE PUBLIC LIBRARY ON ELM STREET, 1909. (NHFPL)

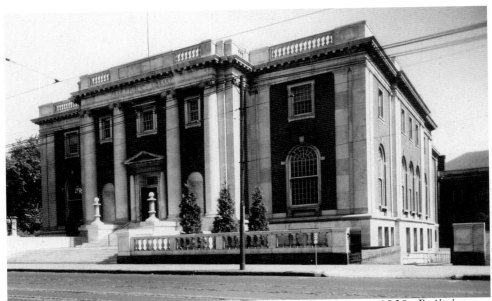

NEW HAVEN FREE PUBLIC LIBRARY ON ELM STREET, C. 1930. Built between 1908 and 1911, Cass Gilbert designed the library in the Neo-Classical and Colonial Revival style to harmonize with the churches on the Green. (NHFPL)

STATE CIRCUIT COURT AND NEW HAVEN FREE PUBLIC LIBRARY ON ELM STREET, C. 1940. *Like the library, William H. Allen and Richard Williams designed the Neo-Classical courthouse to harmonize with the churches on the Green. (NHFPL)*

UNION STATION. *Built by Cass Gilbert in 1918, Herbert S. Newman recently renovated the railroad station, restoring it to its former grandeur. (NHFPL)*

PANORAMIC VIEW, CHARLES A. FERRY'S YALE BOWL AFTER IT WAS BUILT IN 1914. The game was between Harvard and Yale with Harvard winning 36 to 0. (YUL)

NEW HAVEN GREEN, C. 1900. (NHFPL)

NEW HAVEN GREEN, C. 1900. (NHFPL)

YALE STUDENT IN THE HARKNESS MEMORIAL QUADRANGLE, 1931. (NHFPL)

AERIAL VIEW OF HINDENBURG OVER NEW HAVEN, MAY 6, 1937, ON ITS
FATEFUL VOYAGE FROM FRANKFORT, GERMANY, TO LAKEHURST, NEW JERSEY.
*The following day, the stern of the zeppelin caught fire and enveloped the airship in flames
above the Lakehurst Naval Air Station. (YUL)*

SOLDIERS PARADING ON THE NEW HAVEN GREEN DURING WORLD WAR II.
Since the beginning of the colonial period, soldiers have paraded and drilled on the Green
during times of war. (NHFPL)

MAJOR A. GLENN MILLER'S MONUMENT IN THE GROVE STREET CEMETERY. Stationed with the 418th AAFTTC Band at Yale University, Miller's aircraft disappeared over the English Channel in late 1944.

EAST ROCK ROAD BRIDGE OVER MILL RIVER, EAST ROCK PARK. (NHFPL)

VIEW OF DIXWELL AVENUE FROM BROADWAY, C. 1950. During the first half of the twentieth century, many black New Haven residents moved from the Oak Street area to a twenty-block area along Dixwell Avenue. (NHFPL)

UNION TRUST COMPANY ON THE CORNER OF CHURCH AND ELM STREETS. The library and courthouse are in the foreground. (NHFPL)

REDEVELOPMENT OF DOWNTOWN, CHURCH STREET, 1959. *This photo was taken during the second phase of Mayor Richard Charles Lee's urban renewal program. (NHFPL)*

GEORGE STREET WITH REDEVELOPMENT OF DOWNTOWN CHURCH STREET IN THE BACKGROUND, 1959. *This photo was taken during the second phase of Mayor Richard Charles Lee's urban renewal program. (NHFPL)*

"HUMAN RIGHTS NOT VIOLENCE" TAGS WORN BY YOUNG BOYS AT THE 1970 MAY DAY DEMONSTRATION ON THE NEW HAVEN GREEN. The rally was held on the first weekend of May to support the release of Black Panther Party members who had been arrested for the murder of Alex Rackley and to prostest the Vietnam War. (YUL)

PRESIDENT JOHN F. KENNEDY. *He is shown with Yale President A. Whitney Griswold, and New Haven Mayor Richard Charles Lee in a motorcade in front of Sterling Memorial Library. Kennedy received an honorary Doctor of Laws degree at Yale's 261st Commencement, 1962. (YUL)*

VIEW OF QUINNIPIAC RIVER NORTH OF GRAND AVENUE. Recently Joel Schiavone has begun to restore the historical—yet neglected—east side of the Quinnipiac River in the Fair Haven Heights neighborhood. (NHFPL)

VIEW OF NEW HAVEN INDUSTRY LOOKING TOWARDS THE HARBOR FROM CHURCH AND CHAPEL STREETS AFTER 1900. The city still has not taken full advantage of its harbor front, transforming it into a vibrant commercial and cultural center for tourism and the public. (NHFPL)

POSTCARD OF CHILDREN ICE SKATING ON THE LOWER GREEN, C. 1907. *During the second half of the nineteenth and part of the twentieth century, children and families skated on the lower end of the Green. Today the New Haven Fire Department no longer floods the southeast corner of the Green, ending one of the city's earlier traditions. (NHFPL)*

THE FRANKLIN ELM ON THE CORNER OF CHAPEL AND CHURCH STREETS. *It was planted on April 17, 1790, to commemorate Benjamin Franklin, the American revolutionary hero who had died that same day. The city removed the tree in 1904 after it fell victim to elm disease. (NHFPL)*

The Civil War and the Road to Prosperity

Continued from page 64

County Superior Court before commanding the Second Regiment of Volunteers and Jackson's Seventh, was promoted to brigadier general after the battles at Port Royal and at Fort Pulaski, Georgia. He also participated in skirmishes around Hilton Head, Morris Island, and James Island, and successfully led an assault on Fort Fisher in North Carolina. By the end of the war Congress had appointed him brigadier general of the regular army and he held the rank of major general of the volunteers. He pursued a military career after the war and led the assault against the Sioux Indians in 1876, in which General George A. Custer fell mortally wounded at Little Big Horn. After being promoted to major general of the regular army in 1886, Terry retired to civilian life in New Haven, where he died in 1890.

Andrew Hull Foote, born in New Haven in 1806, graduated from West Point and, after serving as a midshipman and commander of the *Portsmouth* in the East India Squadron, was placed in charge of the Brooklyn Navy Yard. When the Civil War broke out he received command of the naval forces in the upper Mississippi River and, together with Brigadier-General Ulysses S. Grant, blocked Confederate supplies from the west and southwest. During 1862 he successfully led the gunboat flotilla against Fort Henry, Fort Donelson, and Island No. 10, and was promoted to rear admiral on June 16. Around this time his health quickly deteriorated, the result of a wound he had received at Fort Donelson. He was soon placed in charge of equipment and recruiting in Washington, D.C. Dissatisfied with shore duty, he spoke with Gideon Welles, Secretary of the Navy, and received command of the South Atlantic Blockading Squadron off Charleston, but died en route to take over his new command on June 26, 1863.

When Generals Robert E. Lee and Ulysses S. Grant met at Appomattox Courthouse to end hostilities on April 9, 1865, New Haven had contributed approximately $30 million and 3,000 men to the war effort, of whom 420 were now among the dead. The State Hospital, established in 1826–1827 (and later renamed the New Haven Hospital and eventually Yale-New Haven Hospital), erected a new building for the wounded, which the federal government took over in 1863 and called "The Knight" after one of New Haven's leading physicians.

The National Banking Act of 1862, designed to finance the war effort, led to the establishment of first and second national banks of New Haven, but New Haven's support for the war effort was by no means a unanimous one until the closing months of the war. In the presidential election of 1860, the number of combined Democratic votes for Breckenridge and Douglas were nearly equal to those of Lincoln (a vote of 3,012 to 3,140), and when Democratic candidate General George B. McClellan visited New Haven on the eve of the 1864 presidential election, residents turned up by the thousands to cheer him on. McClellan, who advocated appeasement with the South, lost the election by a close margin, and it was only with the Union successes in Virginia and the assassination of Lincoln the following year that the city became overwhelmingly loyal to the Civil War cause *(see illustration on page 78)*.

New Haven

New Haven's population had now reached over 40,000, having grown from about 4,000 during the revolutionary period and about 11,000 in 1830. Until the mid-1840s immigrants had trickled slowly into New Haven, but with the Potato Famine of 1848, scores of Irish Catholics crossed the Atlantic and settled in the port cities of the northeastern United States. New Haven had experienced earlier Irish immigration—like the Irish laborers who came to work on the Farmington Canal during the 1820s and 1830s and afterwards settled in the area—but nothing on this scale. By 1860, over 7,000 New Haveners were of Irish descent.

As predominantly unskilled and semi-skilled laborers, the Irish worked as common laborers as well as tradesmen, blacksmiths, coppers, and chiselers, and settled in the poorer neighborhoods like Wooster Square, the Hill, and around Grand Avenue in Fair Haven *(see illustration on page 80)*. There they found employment in the carriage factories of Wiswell & Company and F.B. Plumb Company on River Street, and the Bigelow machine factory, also located on River Street after 1869. Hundreds more found employment at the New Haven Clock Company and the Sargent hardware factory, and later many worked on the New Haven railroad.

At first the Irish were well received as a source of cheap labor, but as their numbers grew they were less welcome and soon encountered nativism, namely from their Yankee labor counterparts who were competing in the same job and housing markets. The Know-Nothing Party, which had splintered from the Whig Party and eventually merged into the Republican Party, further fueled anti-Irish sentiment by referring to the "Irish vote" and "the insidious policy of the Church of Rome and all other foreign influences against the institutions of our country." The party's object was clear, as stated in its constitution "to resist" these influences "by placing people, whether by election or appointment, none but native-born Protestant citizens." By 1854, shortly after the first great wave of Irish immigration, New Haven had a Know-Nothing mayor and, between 1855 and 1858, Know-Nothing William T. Minor was governor of the state.

Anti-Catholicism had existed since the Puritans founded New Haven and was still prevalent among Protestant Yankees. When a visiting priest came to the city in 1827 and requested permission to use one of the Protestant chapels for mass, he was greeted with the words, "we have no Popery in New Haven and we don't want any." Five years later, the Irish established the first Catholic church in the Hill section of New Haven, naming it Christ's Church. Having relocated it to the corner of York Street and Davenport Avenue in 1834, they moved it again to Church Street 14 years later, renaming it St. Mary's, and again in 1970 to Hillhouse Avenue *(see illustration on page 80)*. The New Haven *Register* greeted the arrival of the first Catholic church with the headline, "The Pope is Coming!" For many New England Yankees, the Irish were agents of the papacy, servants of "Roman despotism," and consequently they were perceived as a threat to the Protestant establishment.

The Civil War and the Road to Prosperity

At about the same time the Irish were arriving in New England, Bavarian Jews began to arrive in the city bringing with them professional skills and business knowledge. Among the first Bavarian entrepreneurs were Lewis Osterwieiss, who established the New Haven cigar industry; and Max Adler, who together with Isaac and Abraham Strouse established the corset industry in New Haven. As early as 1840 these same immigrants had organized Congregation Mishkan Israel, the first Jewish synagogue in the city, and comprised a large percentage of the 2,000 Germans in New Haven at the beginning of the Civil War.

With the Prussian wars and social upheaval, more German immigrants arrived in New Haven after the Civil War. Skilled and literate, they shared some of the same values and customs with Protestant New Haveners and, as Mark J. Mininberg has pointed out, "never lived in separate ethnic neighborhoods but were spread throughout the city, living in relative harmony with the Yankees." As Lutherans and Catholics, they founded the German Evangelical Lutheran Trinity Church and St. Boniface. They also established the Harugari lodges, breweries, and singing societies. At times they, together with German Jews, experienced episodes of xenophobia and nativism, though never at the same level or intensity as the Irish, whose numbers were much larger and threatened the Yankee establishment.

By 1880 Italians and Eastern Europeans, namely from Russia, were coming to New Haven in large numbers. The former, who were escaping poverty and little opportunity in southern Italy, came to work in New Haven's expanding industry and on the railroad, and settled in the Wooster Square section in what is now the Italian section of the city. There they found employment at the Candee Rubber Boot Company on Greene Street, Sargent and Company on Water Street, and Strouse-Adler on Oak Street. In 1899 they organized St. Michael's Church in Wooster Saquare, the first Italian Catholic parish of New Haven, and then St. Anthony's in 1903. Other Italians, including a number of northern Italians, settled in the Hill section in what the New Haven *Register* on February 3, 1872, described as "the Italian section of the city." There they found employment on the railroad and some even opened up small shops on Oak Street alongside Jewish establishments.

Russian Jews, who were fleeing Czarist pogroms (and who would later flee the Bolshevik uprisings), settled in the Hill section too, living in and around Oak Street as well as along Grand Avenue in the Irish section of Fair Haven. In 1891 they organized B'Nai Jacob, New Haven's second synagogue. Although they were not as well received as the Bavarian Jews—who appeared more westernized to New Haven Yankees—they quickly adapted to economic life in the city. Many found employment as shoemakers, tailors, and blacksmiths, as well as in the Bavarian cigar and corset factories. Others opened small shops on Oak Street dealing in dry goods, clothes, and hardware and some took to street peddling. Charles Reznikoff, whose family had fled Elizavetgrad, Russia, described these new immigrants in the early and late twentieth century:

> Almost all penniless at first, the Jewish immigrants from Eastern Europe made their homes at the center of the city—near lower Congress Avenue—in one of the poorest neighborhoods. . . . They lived in a close community along Oak Street, no more than three blocks of it. . . . Along Oak Street were the stores: merchandise out in front in boxes and barrels or just heaped on the sidewalk. Somewhere along the street, in winter, would be found a man peddling hot sweet potatoes, and, in summer, in front of every grocery was a can of "hot corn" (a penny each until the First World War). . . . Some of the Jews of Oak Street were tailors; there were also shoemakers, blacksmiths, and carpenters among them. Some were peddlers: pushcart peddlers who sold fruit and vegetables from a wagon and "customer peddlers" who carried a pack of dry goods from door to door. Others were dealers in old clothes, rags, and junk. . . . Some of the young men worked for the O.B. North Company, manufactures of hardware for carriages and wagons— and many of the young women worked as sewing-machine operators at corsets, in Strouse-Adler's. And, here and there, minding store, a young fellow . . . might be reading to become a lawyer or doctor in the world beyond Oak Street.

By 1890, over 1,000 Bavarian and Russian Jews were living in New Haven, which grew to about 8,000 by the end of the decade, comprising just under eight percent of the city's population. Simultaneously, the Italian population had grown from about 2,300 to about 7,800, comprising just over seven percent of the city's population.

By 1900, the foreign-born population of New Haven was 28 percent. The Irish, German, Italian, and Russian people comprised a large percent of this number, but other immigrant groups from Canada, England, Scotland, France, Holland, Belgium, Sweden, Denmark, Norway, Austria, Hungary, Turkey, Romania, and Lithuania also populated the city by the close of the century. As their numbers increased, they founded social agencies like the Order of Vasa (Swedish), the Sons of Norway, and the Wreath of the Eagle (Slovak). Similarly, the Irish, Germans, Italians, and Jews founded the Hibernian Provident Association (Irish), the Knights of Columbus (Irish), the Sons of Herman (German), the Sons of Italy, and B'rith Abraham, and all contributed to the city's new cultural identity.

The main factor behind such a large influx of European immigration in the second half of the nineteenth century was industrial growth and greater economic opportunities in the United States. As mentioned in the previous chapter, New Haven's industry had expanded and diversified during the early republic, adopting a variety of methods to produce commodities and goods on a large scale. By the beginning of the Civil War the city had over 230 manufacturers according to Benham's *New Haven Directory* for the year 1860, not to mention a growing oyster industry. The production of carriages was still the city's leading manufacture. By 1857, the city was producing over 7,000 carriages valued at $1.1 million per annum and, according to the 1872 *New Haven Directory*, there were over 40 carriage and carriage parts manufacturers operating in and around the city. Yet there was also a noticeable shift toward heavy industry:

Axles	1	Eyeglasses	2
Belts	1	Paper Boxes	2
Bits	1	Powder Flasks	2
Buckles	1	Pumps	2
Sail Makers	1	Powder Flasks	2
Saws	1	Saddles	2
Builder's Iron	1	Steam Heating	2
Curry Combs	1	Iron Railings	2
Brushes	1	Boilers	3
Daguerreotype Cases	1	Cigar Boxes	3
Coach Lace	1	Carpets	3
Knitting Machines	1	Jewelry	3
Knobs	1	Neck Ties	3
Candles	1	Firearms	3
Coffee Pots	1	Locks	3
Optical Instruments	1	Matches	3
Plows	1	Paper	3
Pianos	1	Paper Boxes	3
Railroad Frogs	1	Washing Machines	3
Railroad Signals	1	Wheels	3
Ivory	1	Window Springs & Fixtures	3
India Rubber	1	Coach Lamps	4
Pocket Books	1	Malleable Iron	4
Varnish	1	Shirts	4
Tape Measures	1	Bolts, Nuts, Screws	5
Water Pipes	1	Machine Tools	5
Whips	1	Brass Foundries	8
Wire	1	Iron	8
Toys	1	Soap	8
Twine	1	Carriage Parts	11
Cutlery	2	Sewing Machines	11
Chairs	2	Watches and Jewelry	14
Carriage Springs	2	Harness and Saddles	17
Perfumes	2	Hardware and Iron	19
Clocks	2	Stoves and Furnaces	21
Horse-Drawn Cars	2	Carriages	30

By the end of the nineteenth century, New Haven was still making high-quality carriages and carriage parts, having won awards at exhibits in Australia (1888), Paris (1889), and Chicago (1893). At the Columbian Exposition in Chicago, five New Haven firms won prizes for their carriages and carriage parts, but their days as a leading manufacturer in New Haven were numbered as the introduction of the automobile annihilated a whole industry across the nation. Only C. Cowles and Company, founded in 1838 by Chandler Cowles and one of the winners of the Columbian Exposition, survived the storm. The manufacturer of fine carriage lanterns restructured itself and began to produce automobile parts, for which it still has a reputation to this day.

Another New Haven industry was hardware. Eli Whitney Blake and his brothers were the first to manufacture domestic hardware in the United States, producing mortised locks and bedstead castors at their Westville plant as early as 1836. Shortly thereafter, Pierpont and Hotchkiss—later the Mallory-Wheeler Company—began to manufacture locks and doorknobs. Davenport and Mallory, another predecessor of the Mallory-Wheeler Company, were producing about 2,000 padlocks a day on the eve of the Civil War and, in 1854, received the acclamation of a British parliamentary commission for its machines that made interchangeable parts. H.B. Ives Company, established in 1876, manufactured mortise bolts and is still a major participant in New Haven industry today. The leader of New Haven hardware, however, emerged a year before the end of the Civil War when Joseph Bradford Sargent and his brothers George and Edward established the Sargent plant at the corner of Water, Wallace, and Hamilton Streets, an industry that is still thriving today on Long Wharf Industrial Park. With a workforce of 160 men, which rose to about 2,000 during the 1870s, Sargent and Company produced a variety of hardware items, including architectural hardware, and was the major producer of locks by the end of the nineteenth century.

The rubber industry was similarly important in New Haven during this period. Between the years 1834 and 1844, Charles Goodyear, a descendent of Stephen Goodyear, perfected and patented the vulcanization process of "India rubber," a process by which rubber retained its elasticity regardless of temperature; that is to say, it prevented rubber from becoming sticky or melting during the hot summers or freezing during the cold winters. The vulcanizing process introduced many commercial possibilities for India rubber and revolutionized the American rubber industry. With Goodyear's patent, Leverett Candee and his partners Henry and Lucius Hotchkiss formed the L. Candee Rubber Company in 1843 and were soon producing rubber shoes and boots for an international market. By 1892, Candee had become the third largest rubber factory in the United States, employing 1,000 workers and merging into the United States Rubber Company that same year.

Other important New Haven industries in the second half of the nineteenth century—besides carriages, firearms, hardware, and rubber—were paper, pulp, paper boxes, matches, and clocks. The first paper mill was built in Westville in 1776, but soon other mills were operating in New Haven. Joseph Parker, for example, opened a paper mill on Whalley Avenue and Dayton Street during the 1840s and installed one of the first Fourdrinier machines to transfer bleached wood pulp to rolls of paper. He developed a reputation for producing high-quality book paper, but perfected a superior type of blotting paper in 1856 for which the mill maintained an excellent reputation until the second half of the twentieth century. By the 1870s, New Haven had three pulp factories as well as two box factories, of which the National Folding Box

Company on James Street was the largest paper box factory in the world by the beginning of the twentieth century.

Thomas Sanford and his partner Anson Beecher made their names as inventors of machines that cut matchsticks, dipped them into a solution of carbon disulphide and phosphorus, and packed them into matchboxes. They also developed a single machine to convert raw lumber into matchboxes. Diamond Match Company, owned by the Beechers, produced large quantities of matches and matchboxes until its removal to Ohio at the end of the century.

As a clockmaker Chauncey Jerome, who opened a factory on Hamilton Street in 1842, was the first mass producer of wooden clocks in New Haven, making them affordable commodities to many middle- and lower-income consumers. After Jerome encountered financial difficulties during the 1850s, James E. English and Hiram Camp of the New Haven Clock Company took control of the company's assets and transformed it into the largest clock manufacturer in Connecticut and one of the largest in the world.

As industry expanded and diversified in the second half of the nineteenth century, New Haven prospered. Great wealth and civic improvements were evident in most quarters. The New Haven *Register* reported in September 1873:

> There is probably not a city in New England whose comparative growth today equals that of New Haven. If it is doubted, get into a carriage, and tell the driver to take a circuit of the suburbs. New streets are opening, new buildings going up, gas and city water in every direction, factories building, and all the signs of rapid and prosperous growth meet the eye at every turn.

Industries covered the landscape, and by 1897 there were 742 different manufacturing concerns, which included 137 major metal industries, 83 paper and printing companies, 65 garment makers, 55 vehicle-related companies, and hundreds of other consumer commodity industries. By 1900 there were, according to the 1900 census of New Haven, over 1,200 manufacturing and mechanical industries (the standard number of manufacturing establishments was somewhere between 200 and 500), employing over 20,500 workers, of whom 15,393 were men, 4,884 were women, and 259 were children under the age of 16, including:

Clothing, Men's, Factory Products	3
Clothing, Women's, Factory Products	3
Electrical Construction and Repairs	3
Dyeing and Cleaning	4
Cars and General Shop Construction and Repairs By Steam Railroad Companies	4
Brass Castings and Brass Finishing	4
Awnings, Tents, and Sails	5
Boxes, Fancy and Paper	6
Carriage and Wagon Materials	6

New Haven

The overall number of industries in this census is higher than later ones because it apparently included mechanical industries like bicycle and shoe repairs, etc.

With a population of about 108,000 inhabitants, New Haven was clearly the largest industrial center in Connecticut with nearly 12 percent of the state's population. It possessed capital for manufacturing in excess of $30 million and a product value in excess of $41 million.

Contributing to this industrial growth was the introduction of steam power and eventually electricity. In the first half of the nineteenth century, manufacturers had relied on waterpower, even after the invention of steam navigation and the railroad. By 1838 only 11 New Haven factories were using steam as a source of power, but by the end of the Civil War most factories were using steam power. The emergence of the railroad was also a gradual development, the result of numerous consolidations and mergers. By 1872 the New York & New Haven Railroad merged with the Hartford & New Haven Railroad and, by 1889, the major railroads in Rhode Island and southern Massachusetts merged with Connecticut to link Boston and New York. By 1890 the New Haven railroad system was generating revenue in excess of $100 million per year and employing 4,000 workers to serve 12 million passengers annually.

New England railroads—unlike those in the west where the railroad preceded and shaped settlement—emerged as a way to link existing towns, businesses, and markets. In the city, however, other modes of transportation emerged as an alternative to the horse-drawn carriage. Horse-drawn "trolleys," which traveled along a network of railway tracks, emerged after 1860 when the Fair Haven and Westville Railroad Company received a charter to build a line between Fair Haven and Westville. The track soon expanded to other sections of the city, linking neighborhoods and businesses and eventually reaching the outer towns of New Haven. The introduction of the horse-drawn trolley not only allowed passengers to live farther away from their place of employment, it provided lower-income groups with affordable transportation, as did the introduction of the bicycle around this time, which quickly caught on and became popular with both students and townsfolk. By 1869 New Haven was experiencing its first bicycle craze, known as "velocipedemania," and soon there were thousands of bicycles in and around the city *(see illustration on page 81)*.

Besides economic prosperity, New Haven had flourished culturally and architecturally and was a city of great beauty and opportunity by the middle of the century. It was now, as author Louisa Tutthill referred to it, "The City of Elms." The planting of elm trees had begun as early as 1759 when 250 buttonwood and elm trees were planted around the Green, and shortly afterwards a line of elm trees was planted along Temple Street in front of the new brick State House (built between 1761 and 1764) and the two churches. In 1790 the city created a committee "to prepare a draft of a Bye-Law for preserving trees for shade and ornament in this City." Around this time James Hillhouse and David Austin began to plant a number of elm trees around New Haven, and in 1790, the same year as Benjamin Franklin's death, the "Franklin Elm" was planted in the southeast corner of the Green *(see illustration on page 100)*. By the end of the century the city passed an ordinance to protect the Green and, as beautification projects continued well into the nineteenth century, New Haven received acknowledgement for its splendor and beauty. As early as 1809 Samuel Woodworth used verse to praise the Elm City for its natural beauty and charm:

> Hail happy mistress of a happy state!
> With blessing chartered by auspicious Fate;
> For whom kind Nature, with a liberal hand,
> From Copia's horn pours plenty o'er the land.
> Here rural charms with city beauties join,
> Here Art and Nature everywhere combine;
> The colonnade, the portico, and tower,
> Rise on the turf that bears a poplar bower . . .

Yale president Timothy Dwight's views were equally complimentary of New Haven when he wrote the following in *Travels in New England and New York* (1822):

> The views in and around this town are delightful. Scenery does not often strike the eyes with more pleasure. A great number of charming rides in its environs add not a little to the pleasure of a residence in New Haven. Take it all in all, I have never seen the place where I would so willingly spend my life.

Environmental and civic improvements continued, so when Simeon Baldwin Jr. returned to New Haven in 1824, he could not help but notice:

> I think I never saw the New Haven look better than it now does— a great many new dwelling houses have been built since I was last there and several stores besides new college building and a chapel, the sidewalks are paved in most of the streets, and an order is out for paving our wharf as far as Forbes store. . . . The work of the past few years is to the credit of the city.

New Haven

In 1833, a group of prominent citizens—committed to the "improvement of architecture and scenery, in the structure of buildings and laying out of grounds, the cultivation of a refined taste, and the permanent embellishment of our city"—organized the Society for Rural and Architectural Improvement. By the 1840s the society was making improvements to the Grove Street Cemetery and setting new architectural trends in and about the city.

New Haven's most prominent architect by mid-century designed an assortment of structures in the city, including the Early Victorian Gothic–style Old Library (now Dwight Hall), Yale's second oldest surviving building (1842), and the front gate to the Grove Street Cemetery (1845), a large entrance with two colonnades and the inscription, "The Dead Shall be Raised." Henry Austin also designed the brownstone City Hall (1862) on Church Street, although some have credited his associate David Russell Brown. Built in the High Victorian Gothic style, Herbert S. Newman and Associates have recently made additions to the structure while preserving the dignity of the old building. The brownstone County Courthouse (1872), built next to City Hall on Court Street, was also in the Gothic style and was later replaced by a neo-classical courthouse on the corner of Church and Elm Streets. New Haven's architectural renaissance, however, was set back in 1889 by the loss of one of its treasures. After the city ceased to be the co-capital of Connecticut in 1873, Ithiel Town's Greek Revival Statehouse on the Green fell into disrepair and was pulled down over the protests of many citizens *(see illustrations on page 79)*.

As industry emerged in the nineteenth century and smokestacks began to litter the landscape and horizon, New Haveners remained committed to the environment. They preserved greenbelts and parks and developed new ones, like Brewster Park (later Hamilton Park) on Whalley Avenue and Norton Street *(see illustrations on pages 82 and 84)*, so when Harriett Terry, the sister of Major-General Terry, wrote to her sisters in 1887 she could boast that the city

> never was so beautiful. I do not mean that it is merely more beautiful to my eyes, but it is actually more beautiful than ever. The trees have grown and are kept in perfect condition, no worms, even in June, and the streets are clean as they can be, while the passion for ornamenting private grounds of any size. It is without question the prettiest town I was ever in.

By mid-century, the success of Central Park in New York City led to further preservation projects in New Haven. Some were private enterprises like Edgewood farm, which came about after Donald Grant Mitchell—also known by his penname Ika Marvel—bought a 360-acre farm in Westville and turned it into a public park in 1889. Edgewood attracted New Haven's intellectual elite and visitors came from all different parts of the United States to see its splendor and beauty. Other parks emerged as well, including East Rock, West Rock, Fort Hale, Waterside, and Bayview. Mitchell's watercolors served as blueprints for their design and future parkway developments in the late nineteenth and early twentieth centuries. Mitchell, unlike the post–World War II view of suburban escapism, envisaged the coexistence of urban and rural life. In his essay "Highways and Parks" (1884), he expressed this vision:

> [The ideal city] should have its little nucleus of business quarters upon a bay, or a river . . . and this business nucleus crystallizing there under the compression of an outlying circle of green, jealously guarded, would project its rays, or avenues of traffic athwart this circle; and those avenues of traffic, by their accretions of lesser and lighter business, would demand zebra-like cross-bars of space and greenness and foliage, to be flanked with files of houses such that a man could not go to work without sight of trees, or a chance to put his foot to the live earth; while all schools and courts and hospitals should have their setting of green.

The symbiosis of rural and urban life, as Mitchell envisaged it, was New Haven's blueprint for the next century.

Economic and cultural prosperity included social change regardless of gender, race, or class. Indeed, during the second half of the nineteenth century women took major steps toward social and political equality. The Civil War had forced many married women to run their husbands' businesses while their spouses served in the Union army. Other women made soap and mattresses for the soldiers. Yet others, who appear to have been less economically independent, simply worked to support themselves and their families. These women comprised a large segment of the city's labor force and earned lower wages. In 1860, as Ira M. Leonard has pointed out, they "accounted for 40 percent of the 8,000 persons employed in the town's various manufacturing establishments." By the end of the century, they accounted for about 25 percent of the labor force, earning one-sixth of the average man's wage.

After the Civil War, some single women from New Haven traveled south where they worked as teachers among the newly-emancipated slaves. Others worked as government clerks, nurses, and fund-raisers. In 1867, lecturer and writer Frances Ellen Burr brought a petition for women's suffrage to the Connecticut legislature, which was defeated by a vote of 111 to 93. The 18-vote margin encouraged other women to fight for political equality and, in 1869, Susan B. Anthony and Isabella Beecher Hooker founded the Connecticut Women Suffrage Association.

The following year New Haven's first woman minister, Phoebe Hanaford of the Universalist Church, opened the session of the state legislature at New Haven, where another petition was defeated. The first local suffrage committee was organized a year later, attracting socially prominent women, Yale professors, and even businessmen. In 1893, the Suffrage Association won its first major victory when the state legislature allowed women to vote in school-board elections. The movement won other victories including equal guardianship for children, the raising of the age of consent, and the married women's property act, but women did not receive the political franchise until 1920 when Congress amended the federal Constitution to include women.

Another area where women improved their social standing in the nineteenth century was in the area of education. By the 1870s, all-male colleges began to accept women, and even Yale considered the possibility of becoming a coeducational institution, though it never adopted the measure until almost a century later. Women, nonetheless, had attended popular lecture series at Yale College as early as 1808 when Professor Benjamin Silliman allowed gifted women to attend his chemistry course. They also attended the recently established School of Art and, in 1892, the Yale Corporation voted to allow women to attend the Graduate School. Soon they were attending the School of Music, established in 1894, but it would take another 75 years before they were allowed to attend as undergraduates.

As discussed earlier, New Haven had erected the first "colored school" in 1811, but when public schools were introduced there were only two primary schools for African Americans and one integrated charity school. One of the students of Sally Wilson's Artisan Street Colored School was Edward Bouchet, the son of an African slave. In 1876 he completed his Ph.D. degree at Yale College, becoming the first African American to earn a doctorate degree in the United States.

In 1824, Bouchet's father had come from Charleston, South Carolina to New Haven as the "body servant" of John B. Robertson, a Yale freshman. Both men stayed on in New Haven and, in 1852, Edward Bouchet was born, attending a charity school and graduating from Hopkins Grammar School as valedictorian. He then attended Yale College, graduating with highest honors and a member of the Phi Beta Kappa Society. As the college's first African-American graduate, he went on to study science at the Yale Graduate School where he earned a Ph.D. degree on the centennial year of the Declaration of Independence. Afterwards Bouchet went to Philadelphia where he became a teacher and was an active member of the NAACP. He eventually returned to New Haven, where he died in 1918 and was buried in the Evergreen Cemetery.

During the 1870s Yale also received a generous bequest from Mary Goodman, an African-American resident, who left her entire estate to fund a scholarship for African-American students in the Yale Divinity School. In all, she left $5,000. The Yale Corporation, recognizing her great contribution, had her buried in the college lot of the Grove Street Cemetery, where the following inscription can be found on her tombstone: "Mary A. Goodman, of African descent, who gave the earnings of her life to educate men of her own color in Yale College for the Gospel ministry." The scholarship survives today and is a testimony to the Goodman name.

Yale College, in turn, brought many social benefits to the Elm City. Between 1870 and 1900, its student and faculty body grew from 819 to 2,944, becoming one of the largest universities in the United States. Many small shops and businesses emerged to cater to student and faculty needs. Local residents, moreover, found employment at the university as it continued to grow throughout the twentieth century, becoming New Haven's largest employer by the end of that century.

But friction also existed between town and gown. In 1812, townsfolk and students clashed in a large fight involving clubs and knives. In 1824, townies who suspected Yale medical students of grave-robbing attacked the Medical School (established in 1813) after a rumor spread that students had snatched a dead woman's body from a West Haven cemetery. In 1854 a group of 50 to 60 students clashed with townies on the Green, close to College Street. Students, who carried pistols with them, fired upon the crowd that was throwing bricks from a nearby construction site. In the tumult, a student stabbed and killed the townie leader, Patrick O'Neill. Four years later, in a scuffle with a local fire company, a student fatally wounded a fireman with his pistol. In both cases, no one was held responsible, but thereafter President Theodore Dwight Woolsey prohibited students from carrying weapons. The remainder of the nineteenth century was less violent, but tensions between town and gown persisted into the twentieth century when two more town-gown battles took place, resulting in many injuries (see illustration on page 83).

With population and industrial growth in the nineteenth century, preservation of social order became more requisite. New Haven had long relied on a volunteer constable system and an organized Night Watch, which was reorganized after the mail robbery of 1820 to include a body of 50 part-time law enforcers. According to the ordinance of January 13, the city provided for "the appointment of seven discreet citizens to act as superintendents of the watch and not to exceed fifty citizens to act as watchmen." The night watchmen worked from dusk until dawn, taking the Sabbath off, and were allowed to carry a "staff" about three feet long.

Town disorders, student rioting, and fire lootings demanded a more professional service. In May 1861 Mayor Harmanus Welch instituted the first regular police department under the authority of the state legislature, which called for a six-man board of police commissioners, the mayor to serve as general chairman and a member ex-officio, a chief of police, one captain, one lieutenant, fourteen patrolmen, and fifteen "supers" or supernumeraries. The first chief of police was Jonathan W. Pond. Wales French served as captain and Owen Munson as lieutenant, and another 12 police officers were added to the force. Two months after the board of police commissioners met for the first time on July 6, they introduced a uniform consisting of blue coats and "trousers," a shield bearing the city's coat of arms, and an English bobbie-style helmet, "bell-crowned and of imposing size." By 1872, the number of police officers had increased to 85, and two years later, the New Haven Police Department moved into the first floor of the newly-built city courthouse on Court Street in Fair Haven.

Chapter Five

THE TWENTIETH CENTURY AND THE END OF PROSPERITY

During the colonial period, New Haven had struggled to become a successful commercial center along the North American seaboard. Having failed to establish a direct trade route with England during the 1640s, its ventures into the Delaware and other parts of New England to partake in the fur trade proved to be equally non-profitable. By the early republic, however, New Haven emerged as one of the leading manufacturing centers of the United States. Ironically the small Puritan town, which had failed to become an economic success during the colonial period, had become just that. "A Yankee community," as William Johnston described it, "was about to be overwhelmed, numerically at least, by a polyglot of waves of Germans, Irish, Russians, Italians, and—later—Blacks," and with them "came languages, religions, tastes and opinions foreign to what had been known as 'the land of steady habits.' "

With industrialization, New Haven's population grew nearly tenfold during the course of the nineteenth century. In 1840, its population was about 13,000; at the outbreak of the Civil War, it was about 40,000; and by the turn of the century it was about 108,000. Many of these new citizens were from Europe, having migrated from Ireland, Italy, Germany, and Eastern Europe. America's political stability and growing industry provided many with political and economic opportunity, so by 1900 almost one-third of the city's population was foreign-born. As the *Saturday Chronicle* reported on November 21, 1903, "The character of the population of this city has changed not a little in the past twenty years. In 1880, the total population in New Haven was 62,882. In 1900, there were 60,159 of foreign parentage." And a decade later, at least one-third of the population was foreign-born, another third had at least one immigrant parent, and only 28.2 percent of the population—comprising 37,726 residents—had two white native-born parents. This demographic trend continued, so that by 1930 the number of foreign-born and those of foreign parentage had risen to about 70 percent of the city's total population.

At the turn of the century the Irish were still the largest foreign-born group in the city. Having comprised one-fifth to one-quarter of the city's population at the outbreak of the Civil War, their numbers grew smaller in proportion to other immigrant groups by the early years of the twentieth century. The census of 1910, for example, placed them at 9,004, comprising less than seven percent of the city's population. By 1930 they constituted about 25,000, becoming the second largest ethnic group in the city. The Italian population on the other hand, which had constituted no more than 10 residents in 1870, grew dramatically by the close of the century. Between 1890 and 1900, 3,386 Italians settled in New Haven. The following decade another 7,897 arrived and the New Haven Italian community, both foreign-born and of foreign parentage, grew to 13,159. By 1930 Italians were the city's largest ethnic group and an important voting bloc, numbering 41,858 residents and constituting over 25 percent of the population. No longer were the old Protestant Yankees the majority, as indicated by a 1930s survey found in Jerome K. Myers's *The Differential Time Factor in Assimilation: A Study of Aspects and Processes of Assimilation among the Italians of New Haven*:

New Haven Ethnic Groups

Italians	50,000	Germans	19,000
Irish	35,000	Polish	6,000
Jews (mostly Russian)	25,000	African Americans	5,300
British-Americans	20,000	Scandinavians	3,500

The above statistics include native-born of mixed-foreign parentage, so the totals are higher in some instances. A decade later, Italians still constituted a quarter of the city's population while the Irish made up an eighth, the Russian and Polish another eighth, and the Germans and Scandinavians a sixteenth.

Unlike the Irish, the first generation of Italian immigrants did not come to New Haven with a tradition of political involvement. Originating largely from rural southern Italy where only two percent of the population could vote before 1882 and only seven percent after 1913, and where heavy taxes burdened the mainly poor population, they tended to be suspicious of governments. There "grew up in the south of Italy," as Morty Miller has described it, "a tradition of opposition to civil authority, a code of non-cooperation with the government." This tradition carried over to New Haven, where newly-arrived Italians refrained from entering political life while a small group, who escaped Connecticut's English-literacy voting requirements, tended to support the Democratic Party and an Irish political leadership.

As their numbers grew, however, Italians increasingly partook in the political process, numbering 4,000 voters by 1910. Four years earlier, Antonio Vannacori won the first Italian seat on the Board of Alderman, and for each successive year an Italian has held the fifth (later the tenth) ward. By the early 1920s, Republican Lorenzo Furcolo and Democrat Anthony Adinolfi had won seats in the State Senate, and after World War II, Republican William C. Celentano became the city's first mayor of Italian descent. The Republican Party, having realized the importance of the growing Italian vote, organized a campaign under the Ullman brothers to win over the new vote. Consequently, Italians tended to favor both parties until the 1920s and 1930s when many returned to the Democratic Party, which, as Mark Mininberg has pointed out, was "generally Catholic, foreign-born and lacking much formal education" by 1930. The Republican Party, on the other hand, "was once again the party of the Protestant, Northern

European, and educated classes." Two exceptions, as he acknowledged, were wards 10 and 19, Wooster Square and Dixwell Avenue, which "were holdovers from earlier eras, with some Italians remaining loyal to the Ullman coalition and the Blacks still clinging to the Party of Lincoln." More recently, New Haven had two Democratic mayors: Ben DiLieto, who served five terms after 1979, and John DeStefano, who was elected in 1993 and is still serving as the city's mayor. Rosa Delauro, a New Haven Congresswoman of Italian descent, is also serving in Washington, representing the south-central region of Connecticut.

Whereas the first wave of Italian immigrants avoided entering New Haven political life, the Irish found their political voice within a decade of their arrival during the 1840s. Having learned from their experiences in Britain "that political power was critical to survival in a Protestant world," they quickly organized themselves into a voting bloc, throwing their support behind the Democratic Party. Their first victory came when Thomas Cahill was elected to the Board of Aldermen in 1854 and to the Common Council in 1857. By 1880, the same year the city increased the number of wards from six to twelve, they won six of the twelve aldermen wards and, as supporters of the Democratic Party, ensured that 10 of the 14 mayors from 1860 to 1895 were Democratic. In 1899, Cornelius Driscoll became the first Irish-Catholic mayor of New Haven and for the next 70 years, until Richard Charles Lee left office in 1969, every Democratic mayoral candidate had an Irish-Catholic lineage.

Other ethnic groups also found their political voice in the late nineteenth and early twentieth centuries. The Germans had their first alderman in 1875 when Henry Kettendorf was elected to the board. In 1881 Simon Shoninger, a Bavarian Jew whose father had come from Germany to New Haven and established the B. Shoninger Organ Company, was the first Jew to be elected to the Board of Aldermen. Having escaped Czarist persecution, many Russian Jews avoided political participation while others experimented with socialism. "Some of them, especially the religiously Orthodox," as Irving Howe and Kenneth Libo explained Jews in America at the time, "tended to look upon politics as something . . . dangerous, soiling, a prerogative of the Gentiles. Others, especially the Yiddish-speaking socialists, regarded American politics as vulgar, devoid of seriousness and ideas, a mere device for manipulating the masses."

By 1899 the Russian Jews entered the political arena when brothers Louis and Isaac Ullman, sons of Bavarian Jewish immigrants and co-owners of the Strouse-Adler corset factory, won control of the Republican Party. As successful businessmen, the Ullman brothers were accepted by the Protestant, Yankee business community, and as the sons of immigrants they won many Jewish voters to the Republican Party. With the Bolshevik uprisings, more Jews came to New Haven and their political influence continued, though the Democratic Party eventually won many of the Jewish votes. Numbering approximately 8,000 in 1900, New Haven's Jewish population grew to about 25,000 in 1930, comprising one-sixth of the total population.

The Twentieth Century and the End of Prosperity

While ethnic groups began to find their political voice, women were kept on the sidelines until 1920 when Congress doubled the United States electorate by allowing women the vote. In 1927, Josepha Whitney was elected to the Board of Aldermen and went on to serve as a representative of the state legislature. In 1941, Laura Belle Reed McCoy, a Mohawk Indian who identified herself with the black community, also won a seat on the board and was the first Democrat to win the Dixwell 19th ward.

During the nineteenth century, immigrant labor had helped New Haven become a leading producer of clocks, plows, wagons, guns, and clothing, among an assortment of other manufacturing goods. However, after World War I, anti-immigration laws reduced the flow of European immigration. Yet at the same time, another source of immigration came from within the United States, as southern blacks and later Hispanics from Puerto Rico settled in the New Haven area. This new influx of black immigrants, as William Johnston described it:

> meant that in 1940 there were about 5,000 Blacks in New Haven. But a decade later the figure had doubled. By 1960 it doubled again. The old points of origin in North Carolina continued to provide a number of new residents, but these were joined by migrants from other cities most notably New York. Once again, a large, unorganized group of new people somehow had to be brought into the community.

But southern black migration had occurred a century earlier when New Haveners complained about the increase of free blacks living "on the outskirts of the city." In 1820, a *Connecticut Herald* editorial expressed a view shared by many white New Haveners: "It is the policy of the slave-holding States to exclude free blacks. They of course come northward and are rapidly increasing in this town. If means for their expulsion be not soon adopted, we shall have them for the winter, and they were imperceptibly become inhabitants." Such migrations were small and in some cases temporary, but after the Civil War their numbers grew as southern-born African Americans came to work as laborers, many finding low-end jobs on the Boulevard Sewer Project during the 1890s. A small but steady flow of West Indians, from Nevis and Jamaica, also arrived in the city by the early 1900s. Their numbers, however, never matched the later migrations from the South.

The first major wave of black migration from the South occurred after World War I when the Winchester Arms Company suspended its discriminatory hiring practices and encouraged southern blacks to come to New Haven for jobs. Yale University also offered them jobs in its janitorial and dining services. Having come from Virginia, South Carolina, and North Carolina, particularly from a hundred-mile North Carolina strip between Edenton and New Bern and Beaufort, and a few having come from the deeper South, particularly Georgia, southerners accounted for about 30 percent of New Haven's black community by 1930. Sixty percent were northern-born and another eight percent were from the West Indies. The black community had now reached about 5,000, constituting about three percent of the city's population; a decade later it grew to about 10,000, about six percent of the population. By 1960 it was 23,000, about 16 percent of the city's population; and by 1975 it grew again to over 44,000, making African Americans the largest ethnic minority next to Italian Americans, who constituted one-third of the population.

Like all ethnic or immigrant groups whose numbers grow in relation to other groups, New Haven blacks found their political voice, but their inclusion was a long and painful process. In the mainstream of politics they had little representation until after the civil rights movement of the 1960s. William Johnston explained it:

> [They] were "third in line" behind the Irish and Italians. From a practical political standpoint, nobody needed the Blacks. They were relatively few in number, and in any event each of the two major parties was courting a larger ethnic constituency of its own. Blacks must have seemed so firmly bound to the "party of Lincoln" that Republicans could take their support for granted, and Democratic overtures would be fruitless. Black New Haven was the unwanted stepchild of local politics.

Although Charles McLinn had won a seat on the Common Council as early as 1874, even before the word "white" was legally removed from the state Constitution, and James Stewart and Dr. I.N. Porter won seats in 1897, their effect was short-lived. With the redistribution of wards in 1921 making Dixwell the 19th, Republican Harry G. Tolliver was elected the first black alderman of the city. Nonetheless, it was not until demographic growth, the civil rights movement, and a gradual shift toward the Democratic Party that the black community enhanced its political standing in the city. The first major breakthrough came in 1969 when Henry Parker nearly won the mayoral candidacy for the Democratic Party, losing to Bartholomew F. Guida by only about 2,000 votes. That same year six African Americans were elected to the Board of Aldermen, and seven years later Alderman William Jones was elected as the first black New Haven Democratic town chairman, making New Haven's blacks a recognized voting bloc in the community. In 1989, the bloc helped to elect John Daniels New Haven's first black mayor.

Another group of American postwar immigrants who came to New Haven in the first half of the twentieth century were Puerto Rican Hispanics. Between 1934 and 1935, seven Puerto Rican men arrived in New Haven to work at the Winchester manufacturing plant. The first was Gummercindo Del Rio, a general foreman who would go on to found the New Haven Puerto Rican Colony Club and the Puerto Rican Democratic Club. He was soon followed by Arcade Rodrigues and Thomas Bone, solderers; Avelino Mendez, a waxer; Angel Chardon, a mechanic; Antonio Ruiz, a machinist; and Antonio Antuan, a machine fitter. Del Rio encouraged other Hispanic men and their families to find jobs and settle in New Haven. Although their numbers were small in proportion to other immigrant groups, another wave of Puerto Rican immigration occurred after World War II when Puerto Rican veterans stayed on in New Haven and encouraged their families to settle there. Many settled on Dixwell Avenue, Henry Street, Ashmun Street, and Winchester Avenue, and eventually spread out to Fair Haven and the Hill, where many Hispanics live today. More recently other Hispanic groups—namely Mexicans and Cubans— have arrived in the city, but their numbers are less than one-half of the Puerto Rican population, who account for nearly one-eighth of the city's population.

With the post–World War II immigration, the Latino community soon found political representation. In 1969 Jose Martinez became the first Hispanic alderman and, in 1988, Tomas Reyes Jr. became the first Hispanic/African American to serve as president of the Board of Aldermen. Although Hispanics did not become an important voting bloc until the 1970s, their numbers were still growing and, like the Asian community who now account for about 5,000 (at least four percent of the city's population), they will play an ever more important role in the political future of New Haven.

With years of immigration and acculturation, ethnic neighborhoods began to emerge in New Haven. The Italians, who comprised five percent of the city's population at the beginning of the twentieth century, had settled in the Wooster Square neighborhood, replacing the Irish who had once lived there. In the poem "Wooster Square," written by Yale student Sidney Deane, one witnesses the racial, high-brow, Protestant view of Italian settlement in the New Haven area at the turn of the century:

> The sunshine yet on Wooster Square
> Is bright as years and years ago;
> The elms are taller, greener there;
> But Fashion's favor changeth so!
> The glooming Grecian portico,
> The ancient, marred, much-trodden stair
> Forgets the days of long-ago,
> Forgets the days of Wooster Square.
>
> The old white church in Wooster Square
> Where godly people met and prayed—
> Dear Souls! they worship Mary there,
> Italian mother, man and maid
> In gaudy Southern scarfs arrayed;
> The horrid candles smoulder where
> The godly people met and prayed.
> Alas! the fall of Wooster Square!
>
> Before the war, in Wooster Square,
> The carriages, they went and came;
> The common folk used wait and stare,
> They bowed to Beauty and to Fame.

And then it ceased to be the same;
The doors are tarnished all and bare
Where shone each colonial name
Departed now from Wooster Square.

O Fashion, fled from Wooster Square
And tripping fast up Prospect Hill
Where orioles flame through fragrant air,
Where daises light the roadside still,
What fickle fancy made you care
To take the way of Prospect Hill,
To leave the walks of Wooster Square?

Be done, be done with tiresome rhymes!
I go with Fortune and Fair,
I owe no love to by-gone times—
Peace to the shades of Wooster Square!

Other Italians settled in the Hill section around Oak Street, in what was clearly one of the least desirable neighborhoods in all of New Haven. During the first wave of mass European immigration, Irish and Germans settled in the Hill section. They were soon replaced by Italians and Russian Jews, who were living in crowded, dilapidated housing and paying in the year 1901, according to a Lowell House survey, "$7 to $13 a month for 2 to 4 rooms" and "one toilet for six families."

Despite New Haven's prosperity as an industrial center during the late nineteenth and early twentieth centuries, slum conditions emerged and defined certain ethnic neighborhoods. Sinclair Lewis from the Yale class of 1907 described Oak Street in his short story "Young Man Axelbord." Having reached the Yale campus at five in the morning, characters Gil and Knute strolled

arm in arm down Chapel Street in search of a restaurant suitable to poets. They were all closed. "The Ghetto will be awake by now," said Gil. "We'll go buy some eats and taken 'em up to my room . . ." Down on Oak Street, a place of low shops, smoky lights and alley mouths, they found the slum already astir. Gil contrived to purchase boxed biscuits, cream cheese, chicken-loaf, a bottle of cream. While Gil was chaffering, Knute stared out into the street milkily lighted by wavering gas and the first feebleness of coming day; he gazed upon Kosher signs and advertisements in Russian letters, shawled women and bearded rabbis; and as he looked he gathered contentment which he could never lose. He had traveled abroad tonight.

African Americans, and later Hispanics, also experienced these slum conditions. As the transformation from slavery to freedom did not bring the economic and social benefits attached to the city's industrial growth, African Americans continued to receive low-end jobs and live in the worst areas of the city by the turn of the century, including the Hill section. Finding it difficult to move to the white-dominated ethnic neighborhoods or white suburbs, they were confined to the poorer neighborhoods close to the city's core. Gradually, many left the Oak Street area for a 20-block area along Dixwell Avenue, northwest of the Green *(see illustration on page 94)*. During the 1950s and 1960s many families moved to Newhallville, a working-class neighborhood where there is still a large black community today. As Robert A. Warner pointed out in his study of *New Haven Negroes* (1940), slum conditions existed in Dixwell and other African-American neighborhoods, and although New Haven's blacks experienced educational equality and residential freedom during the early part of the twentieth century, they were still deprived of economic opportunity. The following chart is from Yohuru Williams's *Black Politics/White Power: Civil Rights, Black Power, and the Black Panthers in New Haven.*

Racial Composition of New Haven Neighborhoods in 1966

Neighborhood	Population	% White	% Black	% Puerto Rican
The Hill	23,000	49.9	42.5	7.6
Dwight	8,000	48.0	50.1	1.9
Dixwell	6,000	10.5	85.1	4.4
Newhallville	10,000	24.2	74.5	1.3
Fairhaven	14,000	59.1	35.5	5.4

Despite the emergence of these slum conditions around the city center, certain private citizens still devoted their time and energy to civic improvements. After Donald Grant Mitchell died in 1908, George Dudley Seymour, a patent lawyer and former resident of Bristol and Hartford, took the lead in developing the green spaces and restoring public buildings. He founded parkways in and around the city, from which there sprung Norton Parkway, Edgewood Parkway, Tower Parkway, and Saltonstall Parkway. Having received President William Howard Taft's assistance in purchasing Fort Hale and Lighthouse Parks, he increased New Haven's parklands and was responsible for the restoration of public and private buildings. Seymour influenced the construction of James Gamble Rogers's Post Office and Federal District Court on Church Street, and William H. Allen and Richard Williams's County Courthouse (now State Circuit Court), all in the Neo-Classical style, as well as Cass Gilbert's Neo-Classical and Colonial Revival Public Library on Elm Street, and Cross and Cross's Colonial Revival Union and New Haven Trust Company (now Union Trust Company) on the corner of Church and Elm Streets *(see illustrations on pages 86–87)*.

For George Seymour, New Haven's beautification was more than a cultural or aesthetic achievement; it had social benefits as well. "When all citizens," as he told the mayor, aldermen, and city residents in an open letter published in the New Haven *Register* on June 2, 1907, "feel that they can enjoy, not by sufferance, but as a matter of right, such privileges as the place affords, the citizens will begin to participate not merely in the privileges, but in obligations of the community, and many of our perplexing problems of municipal government will have disappeared." In his attempts "To Make New Haven City Beautiful," Seymour convinced Yale to open the Peabody Museum and Art Gallery to the public on Sunday afternoons, and persuaded Mayor John P. Studley to appoint a civic improvements committee and commission a report from architect Cass Gilbert and landscape planner Frederick Law Olmsted Jr., whose father had been instrumental in the development of New York City's Central Park (1857) and the Boston Park System (1875–1890). The report, concluded in 1910, advocated the widening of city streets, creating more parks, building a new railroad station, and the serious redevelopment of the harbor. The city officials did not act on these proposals, but gradually they adopted them as more citizens became concerned about urban development. By 1918, Cass Gilbert had designed and built Union Station on Union Street while the university added more buildings around the city, including Woolsey Hall (1901–1902) on the corner of College and Grove Streets and the Yale Bowl (1914), a 64,000-seat stadium located in Westville *(see illustration on page 88)*.

Seymour, who had taken on the cause "to save the elm trees" in 1909, also convinced the city to appoint a superintendent of trees. In a series of open letters in the *Register*, which he began on Sunday, March 21, Seymour reminded the citizens of New Haven of their environmental responsibility to the city:

> The failure of the recent appeal made by Professor Henry S. Graves, director of the Yale Forest School, to the Citizens of New Haven to form a shade tree association leads me to prepare for presentation to the public material that I have been collecting for many months . . .
>
> My objects are:
>
> First, to induce all citizens owning trees at once to notify Professor Graves of their desire to join his proposed association; and second, to induce all citizens who have the welfare of the city at heart to demand the employment by the city of a tree expert, who shall henceforth have the entire care of the existing trees and whose duty it shall be at once to begin systematic planting, this demand to be expressed through the Aldermen or other city officials, through the press, or in any other way.

Seymour wrote two more open letters outlining the history of planting elm trees in New Haven and their subsequent destruction and neglect, first by the canker worm and elm leaf beetle and second by the citizens' neglect and indifference after the great wind storm of 1893, and eventually by Dutch Elm disease. By August, the state legislature had amended the city's charter to include "a bureau of trees in the department of public works" and the appointment of "a superintendent of trees." A year and a half later, George Alexander Cromie, a Canadian native and graduate of the Yale School of Forestry, became the city's first superintendent. Ten thousand trees—including maples, sycamores, lindens, and elms—were planted in and around the city between 1911 and 1921. At the same time, however, 5,000 damaged and diseased trees, mostly elms, were removed, resulting in the loss of many trees on and around the Green *(see illustrations on pages 88 and 89)*.

Seymour, though dying with the thought that his attempts at promoting civic improvements and "the redemption of the harbor" had failed, inspired many civic improvements in the early 1900s and portended a more ambitious urban program during the 1950s and 1960s when Richard Charles Lee would make urban renewal the cornerstone of his political administration. Moreover, he continued the tradition of preserving and developing green spaces in New Haven. By 1900, West Rock, East Rock, Edgewood, and Waterside Parks were the main parks; by the 1970s, there were several more while the city boasted 2,500 acres of public parkland in a city with less than 14,500 acres of total land space. In addition, there were 28 parks, 48 playgrounds, 53 tennis courts, 3 ice-skating rinks, 45 ball fields, and a 15,000-seat stadium.

Other improvements were in the area of higher education. Although a special relationship between Yale University and the city had existed since the colonial period, other institutions were beginning to emerge after World War I. In 1920, for example, the New Haven YMCA (later the University of New Haven) opened as a branch of Northeastern University, and was awarding bachelor and graduate degrees by the 1960s. They now have a student population of over 4,500. Five years later, the Dominican Sisters founded Albertus Magnus College, a Catholic liberal-arts college for women that only recently became a coeducational institution and now has an enrolment of nearly 2,500 students. The Connecticut College of Commerce (later Quinnipiac College and now located in Hamden with over 6,500 students) was founded in 1929 and was awarding bachelor degrees by the second half of the century. Southern Connecticut State University, which emerged from a training school for teachers (1893), became a multi-functional undergraduate and graduate institution during this period and now has an enrollment of over 12,000 students.

With regard to industry, the trend toward heavy industry continued with more foundry and machine-shop products. At the same time, industry became more diverse and new electrical-related products like the refrigerator, and new automobile-related products replaced the dying carriage industry. By the turn of the century New Haven was the most important manufacturing center in Connecticut, and in 1905 it was second only to Bridgeport in the value of its factory products, having invested $31,412,715 in capital *vis-à-vis* a product value of $39,666,118. The principal manufacturers, about 500, were hardware, foundry and machine-shop products, ammunition and firearms, carriages and wagons, malt liquors, paper boxes, and corsets. According to the census of 1909, the number of manufacturing establishments had grown to nearly 600, employing over 25,000 workers, of whom 18,488 were men, 5,778 were women, and 749 were children under the age of 16. These included:

Clocks and Watches 1
Iron and Steel, Steel Works and Rolling Mills 1

New Haven

With a population of approximately 134,000 inhabitants, New Haven industry now held about $52 million in capital investment with a product value of about $51 million. Accompanying the city's population growth and shift towards heavy industry were large government contracts supplying the Spanish-American War (1898–1900), the Philippine Insurgency (1900–1902), World War I (1914–1918), and later World War II (1939–1945). This brought many unskilled and semi-skilled workers and their families to New Haven for war-industry jobs, including African Americans from the South and Hispanics from Puerto Rico. At the same time, a commercial shift toward national chain-owned shopping outlets during the 1920s forced a number of smaller family-owned retail businesses out of business, portending New Haven's future. By the

The Twentieth Century and the End of Prosperity

1930s there were three locally-owned department stores—Gamble-Desmond, Edward Malley, and Shartenberg's—and 250 retail grocery stores. By the second half of the century they were closing, while nationally-owned outlets including Sears and later Walmart, established themselves in the suburbs.

World War I and World War II created many war-industry jobs in the city. The Winchester arms factory, for example, was employing about 15,000 workers during the first war. As the government handed out large contracts for munitions, a number of workers migrated to the city, creating a major housing shortage. Many lived outside of the city while working at the Winchester plant. The housing shortage was underscored by an article in the New Haven *Register*, which reported on May 1, 1916, that "scores of workers in Winchester's have been forced to get homes in the suburbs, all along the shore line road." Jobs were plentiful at the Winchester plant, but after the United States declared war on Germany on April 4, 1917, an employee census was taken to remove all German and Austrian workers who had not taken out naturalization papers. Simultaneously, the city followed the orders of the U.S. Department of Justice, and "enemy aliens" were forbidden from living near munitions plants. The streets around the plant were closed to the public.

At the outbreak of the war many Americans, including Yale faculty and New Haven surgeon Dr. William Verdi, found themselves stranded in Europe. Among the stranded was the mayor of New Haven, Frank J. Rice, who made his way from Cologne to Amsterdam, to London, and then aboard a ship from Liverpool to New York. When he arrived in New Haven, opinion over involvement in the war was divided but quickly turned in the direction of supporting the British-French alliance, especially after the Germans sunk the *Lusitania* and *Sussex* and the allies increased their munitions contracts with the city *(see title page illustration)*.

By June 1916, President Woodrow Wilson, who had intended to keep the United States out of the European conflict, ordered the Second Connecticut Regiment, many of whom were from New Haven County, to engage Francisco Villa and his bandits on the Mexican border. The regiment under the command of Colonel Charles F. McCabe of West Cheshire, and later Colonel John Q. Tilson of New Haven, performed patrol duties and maneuvers close to the border, but accomplished little by the time they returned in October 1916. The following April, Congress passed the declaration of war and the Second Regiment—after patrolling bridges, power stations, and key points of the New Haven railroad—merged with the First Connecticut Regiment of Hartford to form the 102nd Infantry, 26th Division. In early 1918, the 102nd went to France, where it suffered many casualties at Seicheprey, Château-Thierry, St. Mihiel, and the Argonne Forest. As part of the infamous "Yankee Division," the 102nd had 9,000 officers and men, of whom 4,150 fell mortally wounded by the end of the war.

With the rise of Hitler and his conquests in the late 1930s, New Haveners once again watched events unfold in Europe with interest and concern. On

New Haven

May 6, 1937, they witnessed the *Hindenburg* soar over New Haven on its fateful voyage to Lakehurst, New Jersey *(see illustration on page 91)*. Many residents living in the city had either fled from Europe or had ancestors who came to the United States from Poland, Russia, Germany, Italy, or Ireland. Many also had family members still there and supported immediate American intervention after Britain declared war on Germany. The nation, however, remained isolationist until the bombing of Pearl Harbor on December 7, 1941, after which President Franklin D. Roosevelt asked Congress to declare war on Japan. Congress approved the request on December 8, and three days later Germany and Italy declared war on the United States.

On January 30, the first and part of the second battalion of the 102nd were sent to the South Pacific. Company A was stationed on Christmas Island, expecting an attack that never came and, by the spring of 1945, preparing for the invasion of the Japanese mainland. Once the battles of the Coral Sea and Midway had ended the threat of a Japanese invasion, members of the 102nd were reassigned to different units, most going to the 25th and 31st Infantry Divisions, which experienced some of the heaviest fighting of the war. The 25th, for example, was sent to the Solomon Islands, where it partook in the battle of Guadalcanal and later participated in the liberation of the Philippines in early 1945. When President Harry Truman made the fateful decision to drop the atom bomb on Hiroshima and Nagasaki to conclude the war, he spared many American lives, including those in Company A who were expecting casualties as high as 80 or 90 percent during the final offensive.

At the beginning of the war New Haven had thrown itself into the war effort. As in World War I, it used the Green for military drills, marches, and parades *(see illustration on page 92)*. Glenn Miller, who had been stationed at Yale University, conducted the Army–Air Force Band there, marching down Elm Street every Friday evening with the 418th and playing at the center of the Green *(see illustration on page 93)*. Winchester and other factories received large government contracts, creating jobs, and kept their plants open 24 hours a day. As men served in the Pacific and in Europe, women kept up the war effort at home by volunteering, as in the previous war, their services to the Red Cross, Woman's Motor Messenger Service, and the Minute Women, among other organizations. Many also volunteered as airplane spotters and many more entered the workforce to replace the shortage of men in the factories. Those with family members in the service hung a flag with a blue star on the window of their homes, while some hung a flag with a gold star to represent the loss of a family member during the war. When there was a shortage of metal, the city pulled up the trolley tracks while households and schools collected tin cans, pots and pans, and newspapers to support the war effort. By the end of the war New Haven industry was thriving while good roads and the popularity of the automobile made it possible to work in the city and live in the suburbs, to travel greater distances from the city center.

The Twentieth Century and the End of Prosperity

The introduction of the automobile had a profound effect on New Haven industry and social life during the twentieth century. In 1896 E.P. Clapp made the first trial run of a gas engine automobile in New Haven by climbing to the summit of East Rock with a car that had no muffler; he had to stop every few miles for water and gas. Two years later W.F. Manross drove his car from Forestville to New Haven's City Hall in 51 minutes at a speed of 32 miles per hour, making the trip without stopping for gas or water. Although the automobile had been invented elsewhere, the city played an important role in its development. New Haven tube-bending companies, for example, built gas engine manifolds to make a more compact engine while John Petrie of New Haven invented the self-starter magneto, making the task of starting the engine much easier.

The introduction of the automobile had great consequences for the carriage industry. In the early twentieth century, the manufacture of carriages ebbed and quickly disappeared. Richard Hegel lamented its demise in a nostalgic tribute:

> No New Havener of the waning nineteenth century had vision to discern the coming of the automobile age which sent the carriage industry into oblivion. New Haven, which had the best chance of achieving the fame which finally crowned Detroit in far away Michigan, did not adapt itself to change and the carriage factories melted away like ice on a sultry day.

But the end of New Haven's carriage industry was more complicated than Hegel's nostalgic tribute to a bygone age. Another and more important factor that brought an end to the city's proudest manufacture of the nineteenth century was the introduction of electricity, which quickly transformed the nation, including modes of industry and transportation. During the second half of the nineteenth century, New Haven industry had invested heavily in steam power and was reluctant to change over to electricity, but by the close of the century, advances in electrical power convinced a number of local industries to adapt to this new source of power. One of the main incentives behind this sudden change of mind was the introduction and success of the electric streetcar. On June 13, 1892, the New Haven & West Haven Railroad operated the first electric trolley in the city, traveling from Campbell Avenue to Savin Rock, then to Church and Chapel Streets, and back to West Haven. Within a few days, the line was offering a regular service and, by the following year, electric streetcars were traveling along State Street and Winchester Avenue.

That same year the Fair Haven and Westville Railroad received a large government contract to build new lines on Ferry and South Quinnipiac Streets in Fair Haven, and on Fountain Street, Central Avenue, Tryon Street, Forest Street, Rock Street, Springside Avenue, and Wintergreen Lake Road in Westville, as well as a line to the summit of West Rock. The contract further stipulated that the company had the right to operate its lines "by means of either cable or the overhead or other electric system, or any other motive power except steam, or may make use in part of each of said systems." At the same time, the New Haven Electric Light Company, established in 1881, received a contract to supply electric lighting to street lamps and public buildings, though most city buildings continued to use gas illumination until the beginning of the twentieth century. By 1899, the New Haven Electric Light Company merged with Bridgeport Electric Light Company to form the United Illuminating Company, and became one of the largest employers in the city.

Electric streetcars, traveling at high speeds of 60 to 70 miles per hour, carried three times more passengers than horse trolleys and connected the surrounding towns with the inner city. They were a commercial success and the New York, New Haven, & Hartford Railroad Company (sometimes called the New Haven Railroad) soon made its move, establishing the Consolidated Railway Company to buy up control of the interurban lines. In 1904, the Consolidated Railway Company made a purchase offer of $8,700,075 for the property, rights, and franchise of the Fair Haven & Westville Railroad, plus an additional $1,664,000 for the property of the Winchester Avenue Railroad. The Fair Haven and Westville Company accepted the generous offer and handed over its assets on May 23.

By 1904, the New Haven Railroad had absorbed over 25 railroad companies and expanded its trackage to over 2,047 miles. Behind these mergers were J.P. Morgan, Charles Mellen, and a group of wealthy New York investors. Morgan, who had installed Mellen as president of the railroad company, made improvements to the railroad system like the electrification of rail lines and the construction of a power-generating plant in Cos Cob, Connecticut, but his ambitious schemes to achieve a complete monopoly of New England transportation—including steamboat lines, trolley companies, and other railroad lines—left the company on the verge of bankruptcy.

Morgan and Mellen paid outrageous prices to consolidate their monopoly. By 1912 they achieved it, operating over 2,000 miles of railroad and trolley track in New York, Connecticut, Rhode Island, and most of southern Massachusetts. They also controlled the coastal shipping companies like the Fall River Line, but their profits were imaginary—the illusion of clever bookkeeping. When Louis Brandeis, a Boston lawyer, conducted an investigation of the railroad's activities in 1907, he found that the overextended railroad was facing financial collapse. His investigation into the railroad's monopoly received little attention until a 1912 investigation and report by the Interstate Commerce Commission (ICC), which appeared after Morgan's death in 1913, proved that he had been correct. A trial followed with the indictment of 21 New Haven directors and Mellen receiving immunity from prosecution in exchange for his testimony.

During World War I, the federal government operated all the national railroads, including the New Haven Railroad. After the war and during the economic upswing of the 1920s, the railroad was returned to private hands and recovered some of its losses under President Edward Pearson. At its peak, in 1929, the company owned and operated 2,131 miles of track throughout New York, Connecticut, Rhode Island, and southern Massachusetts. To compete with the affordability and popularity of the automobile, it formed the New England Transportation Company, which operated a fleet of trucks and buses, but with the onslaught of the Great Depression the company was once again on the verge of financial collapse. In 1935, President Howard S. Palmer filed under section 77 for bankruptcy and the company remained in trusteeship until 1947 when it returned to private hands.

Other New Haven companies headed towards bankruptcy or moved their operations elsewhere during this period. L. Candee Rubber Company, which had merged into the United States Rubber Company in 1892, for example, closed shop in 1929 and moved its operations elsewhere. New Haven Clock Company, employing nearly 2,000 workers during the jubilant 1920s, closed at the end of World War II. Although the Depression years had devastating effects on the entire nation, New Haven, which elected John Murphy as mayor in 1932 for seven terms, suffered less than the rest of the nation, chiefly because Yale University had received generous bequests from John William Sterling and Edward S. Harkness during the 1920s. Plus, the school commenced a massive project that included the building of ten residential colleges (Jonathan Edwards, Branford, Calhoun, Pierson, Davenport, Saybrook, Trumbull, Berkley, Timothy Dwight, and Silliman); professional and graduate schools, such as the Sterling Law Buildings and the Hall of Graduate Studies on Elm and York Streets; John Russell Pope's colossal Payne Whitney Gymnasium (1932) on Tower Parkway, at one time the largest gym complex in the world and now the second largest after the national training facility in Russia; Harkness Hall on Wall Street; and James Gamble Rogers's impressive Sterling Memorial Library on High Street, which has become the second largest university library in the world behind the Widener Library at Harvard University. The project, which was done in the neo-Gothic style in imitation of the organization and architecture of Oxford and Cambridge in England, employed about 1,200 construction workers and craftsmen, of whom 300 worked on the library alone. During this period, Yale also built the Institute of Human Relations, or "I-Wing," of the Sterling Hall of Medicine (1920–1930) in the Neo-Classical style, which it enlarged 50 years later, constructing a bridge between the I-Wing and the Winchester Building of the Yale–New Haven Hospital.

The war industry during World War II kept New Haven's economy afloat after the Depression, but the changing economy and the mass exodus to the suburbs in the postwar years—which were spurred on by a growing middle class, new roads, and the availability of the automobile—brought a new era of unexpected decline and decay.

Chapter Six

DECAY AND RENEWAL

By 1950 New Haven's population base had grown to about 164,000, from about 108,000 in 1900. A decade later it was about 152,000, the beginning of a serious population decline that would affect the city's economic growth until the present day. Among the main contributors to this downward spiral was the exodus of younger families, particularly from middle- and upper-middle-income groups to the suburbs, where they sought better housing and schools, more spacious living, and less crime.

The middle-class exodus to the suburbs was an American phenomenon occurring across the United States, but unlike other cities in New England and the Midwest, New Haven had a series of incorporated towns along its borders, which refused to be absorbed into the urban center. With the charter of 1784 and subsequent amendments to the charter, the city had defined its borders while incorporated towns along its borders formed separate identities. Consolidation or annexation proved to be futile as a large segment of New Haven's population fled to these neighborhoods and communities. The process of urban-suburban growth, so common in the Midwest and elsewhere, did not occur. New Haven, like other Connecticut cities including Hartford, remained a small-to-middle-sized city encircled by layers of prosperous suburban towns and communities.

The suburban exodus was a turning point for New Haven, marking a downward economic spiral, but interestingly enough, the city's population had stabilized and declined as early as the 1920s and 1930s. Indeed, according to the federal census, the city's population began to decline after 1950, but in that same year and afterwards the census began to include Yale students, indicating that the population had been declining as early as the 1930s. That is to say, without Yale students, the city's population in 1950 was 155,924, and 144,255 the following decade, having declined from 160,605 in 1940, and 162,655 in 1930. Ira M. Leonard provides the following chart in "The Rise of Metropolitan New Haven, 1860 to 1980:"

Population Shift during the Twentieth Century according to U.S. Census

	City of New Haven (New Haven Proper)	Greater New Haven (New Haven and Ten Surrounding Towns)	Area Towns (Excl. New Haven)
1900	108,000	133,689	25,689
1910	133,605	145,139	11,525
1920	162,537	205,371	42,834

1930	162,655		233, 656	71,001
1940	160,605		246, 436	85,831
1950	164,443	(155,924)	273,045	108,602
1960	152,048	(144,255)	342,296	190,248
1970	137,707		355,538	217,831
1980	125,787		338,200	212,413
1990	127, 050		373,240	246,190
2000	123,626		375,366	251,740

The ten surrounding towns include Hamden, Woodbridge, West Haven, North Haven, East Haven, Branford, North Branford, Orange, Bethany, and Guilford.

Since the colonial period, New Haven's population had grown on a regular basis; now that changed. High unemployment during the Great Depression meant that workers and families needed to find work elsewhere, which contributed to outer-city migration. Anti-immigration laws further contributed to demographic change, but it was not until the 1950s that a large number of New Haveners moved to the surrounding towns of Hamden, Woodbridge, West Haven, North Haven, East Haven, Branford, North Branford, Orange, Bethany, Guilford, or further abroad.

As middle- and upper-middle-income groups, mostly white, moved to the Connecticut suburbs in large numbers, so did the city's industry and business. In 1947 New Haven had approximately 34,500 manufacturing jobs; by 1980 it had approximately 14,500, having lost a total of 20,000 jobs in this sector. At the same time suburban jobs, not all manufacturing, had increased by nearly 82,000 as factories in search of cheaper production costs relocated to the suburbs or outside the state, and large shopping malls filled the urban landscape replacing small businesses and transferring a large portion of the retail sector to the outskirts of the city.

New Haven's urban decay was both gradual and sudden. The growth and wealth of the nineteenth and early twentieth centuries did not materialize in the new century and, by the 1950s, there were clear signs of urban decay. Slums had emerged in the inner city, and the downtown commercial district was deteriorating rapidly. "To the south of the City Hall was New Haven's downtown area," Allan R. Talbot described in *The Mayor's Game* (1967):

> Above the fake-marble and neon glitter of first-floor shops were story after story of vacancies. The shabbiness of the area proclaimed what building records could document, that there had been little major capital investment in that declining retail section since before World War I. The streets in and around downtown were choked with trucks and cars, some looking in vain for a place to park, others looking for the other end of Route 1, which would take them elsewhere in New England.

Concerns about urban renewal had existed since the beginning of the twentieth century when George Dudley Seymour influenced and organized civic improvements like those mentioned in the previous chapter, but no large-scale redevelopment program had existed until after the Depression and World War II.

The Federal Housing Act of 1949 and the movement to link the Connecticut turnpike to the inner city paved the way for New Haven's first broad-based urban renewal program. Richard Charles Lee, who lost the mayoral election of 1951 by two votes, recalled one particular event of that election to a *New York Times* reporter on September 3, 1967:

> I went into the homes on Oak Street, and they set up block meetings for me, three and four in one night. And I came from one of those homes and sat on the curb, and I was just as sick as a puppy. Why, the smell of that building! It had no electricity, it had no gas, it had kerosene lamps; light had never seen those corridors in several generations. The smells . . . It was just awful, and I got sick. And there, there I really began.

And begin he did.

In the election of 1953 Lee won soundly, and for the next 16 years he was in office he made urban renewal the cornerstone of his political administration. His goals were to curb middle-class emigration, eliminate slums, rehabilitate obsolescent housing, and revitalize the city's economy. In order to do this he turned to Yale professor Maurice Rotival, adopting his urban renewal plan, and hired attorney Edward Logue to manage it. The city also sought government assistance and on a per capita basis it secured more federal funding than any other city in the United States. By the end of the program the city had rebuilt downtown New Haven, which included an office tower facing Chapel Street, a two-story shopping mall, three hotels, and two department stores. It also cleared slum areas with the building of the Oak Street Connector to I-95, the revitalization of the Church Street area, and the building of offices, stores, high-rise apartments, and low-cost housing.

During the first phase of the program, completed in 1959, Lee and his administration turned their attention to the rebuilding of Oak Street, New Haven's worst slum area, and the neighboring downtown district. They leveled the Oak Street area and built the six-lane Oak Street Connector with three exit ramps leading to the Connecticut Turnpike. With access to the downtown area, they turned their attention to the Church Street area, where construction began on the 19-storey Park Plaza Hotel, an office tower, two department stores for Edward Malley Company and R.H. Macy and Company adjoining the new parking garage designed by Paul Rudolph, the Chapel Square Mall, and eventually the Knights of Columbus and Veterans Memorial Coliseum complex designed by Kevin Roche, John Dinkeloo and Associates *(see illustration on page 95)*. They then turned their attention to Wooster Square, a residential area, where they rehabilitated businesses and built a new community school, senior citizens' center, cooperative housing, library, and an inner-city park. At the same time they rehabilitated the Dixwell area, razing

700 slum dwellings to make way for new cooperative housing and new businesses. Along Long Wharf they filled in marshland and attracted a number of businesses by the end of the 1960s, including Sargent and Company, Armstrong Rubber, Blakeslee Construction Company, Giant Shirt Factory, and a Howard Johnson Motel.

By 1967 Lee's administration had won $120 million in federal funding and, by the end of the decade, had received twice that amount from private sources, including almost $17 million from real-estate entrepreneur Roger L. Stevens and $5 million for the building of Macy's department store. At the same time, it received assistance from a number of local and state government social agencies. In 1962, for example, the city received a $2.5-million grant from the Ford Foundation and organized Community Progress, Inc. (CPI), an antipoverty agency that preceded President Lyndon Johnson's Economic Opportunity Act by two years and focused on education and employment. It soon expanded to include a wide "network of services" in inner-city neighborhoods. The state legislature soon established the Department of Community Affairs (DCA) under the Community Development Act of 1967, granting funds for programs and services in the inner cities. As neighborhood advisory councils evolved into corporations, funding quickly devolved from the city to the neighborhoods themselves, and by 1970 there were seven corporate bodies each receiving about two-thirds of their funds from DCA and the remaining third from CPI.

Although the city had built low-income family housing during Franklin D. Roosevelt's administration and, as Ralph Pearson and Linda Wrigley have pointed out, George Dudley Seymour had initiated a city-planning program at the beginning of the twentieth century, Lee's model was on an unprecedented scale and emphasized many aspects of human renewal. Whereas prewar low-income housing had been typically institutional and for the elderly, under Lee's administration it became less institutional, more widespread, and focused on both low- to moderate-income families and the elderly. By 1970 the city had built more housing for low- and moderate-income families than any other city in Connecticut, and more on a per capita basis than any city in New England. According to the New Haven *Handbook on City Government and Services*, in 1970 the city had 707 new housing units, with an additional 105 still under construction, in the Oak Street sector; 71 new housing units, with an additional 421 still under construction, in the Church Street sector; 261 new housing units, with 36 projected for 1971, and 53 new commercial buildings in the Wooster Square sector; 519 new housing units, with 36 projected for 1971, in the Dixwell sector; 318 new housing units, with an additional 200 still under construction, in the Dwight sector; 116 new housing units for the elderly under construction in the Fair Haven sector; and 52 new housing units, with an additional 36 still under construction and another 102 projected for 1971, in the Newhallville sector.

New Haven

Yet despite all these efforts New Haven's population continued to decline and the city experienced further decay as industry and the middle class left the city. Downtown New Haven eventually experienced the closings of Macy's and Malley's department stores, the Park Plaza Hotel, and many longtime businesses. Housing for low-income families improved, but conversely more housing units were destroyed by urban renewal and highway construction than were built during the 1950s and 1960s. The stub of a superhighway, which might have curved around the city instead of into its heart, remained unfinished, leading to later congestion problems in and around the city.

Racial unrest also overshadowed Lee's efforts. On August 19, 1967, racial tensions came to a climax when rioting erupted in the Hill district, then the neighborhoods of Dixwell, Newhallville, and Fair Haven. Groups of African Americans, mostly youths, broke store windows, looted, set buildings on fire, and stoned several fire engines. The riots lasted three nights, and although they were less severe than the black riots of other American cities that summer, they surprised many across the nation who had come to believe that New Haven was a "model city." As one city official told William Borders of the *New York Times* on August 27, "We thought New Haven had accomplished the things other cities are just beginning to strive for." One staff member of the CPI told the same reporter, "You can talk all you want about how wonderful Dick Lee has been, but it doesn't impress the guy in the slums whose kid's been bitten by a rat."

And if the city boasted the highest per capita funding from the federal government, averaging $800 per person, an African-American man returning from his arraignment for his role in the riots had the following response as he looked at his $150-a-month tenement: "Yeah, $800 is my share. But you don't see one dime of it spent on my block."

Three days after the riots, Lee, who always denied that New Haven was a "model city," accepted the Democratic nomination for his eighth mayoral term, expressing his concerns to a crowd of supporters: "The cities in America are in crisis, and New Haven is among those cities. In a decade we have been trying to solve things which have been wrong with urban America for a century or more. Have I failed? Who can tell?"

Racial tensions emerged again in May of 1969 when George Sams, a Black Panther field marshal, came to New Haven with Alex Rackley of the New York chapter of the Black Panther Party and accused his fellow party member of being a police informant. Rackley was bound, interrogated, and tortured. In his history of the New Haven Black Panther Party, Yohuru Williams described the incident as follows:

> Sams denounced Rackley as a police informant and ordered him bound and held for interrogation in the basement of the Panther headquarters. For three days members of the New Haven chapter, under the direction of Sams, tortured and interrogated Rackley in

the cellar of Warren Kimbro's home. While the New Haven police force listened in, members intermittently beat Rackley and doused his body with boiling water in an effort to extract a confession. Sams ordered Ericka Huggins to record the interrogation for national headquarters. That recording would eventually become a key piece of evidence against the New Haven Panthers.

Rackley was then taken to a marshy swamp in Middlefield, about 20 miles from New Haven, and shot once in the head and once fatally in the chest.

At the same time these events were unfolding, Bobby Seale, one of the co-founders of the national Black Panther Party, arrived in New Haven for a speaking engagement at Yale University. The police, suspecting his involvement, had him and eight other party members charged with the murder of Rackley. Many young New Haveners, including Yale students, thought that Bobby Seale and other party members would not receive a fair trial in New Haven. Yale President Kingman Brewster Jr. expressed "skepticism" that black radicals could receive a fair trial anywhere in the United States, prompting U.S. Vice-president Spiro T. Agnew to demand his ouster from office. Tensions grew to a boiling point on the eve of the 1970 May Day weekend demonstration. Connecticut Governor John N. Dempsey called in the National Guard, telling Attorney General John N. Mitchell "of a 'strong possibility.' " The *New York Times* reported on May 1 "that weekend violence in this tense city could not be contained by National Guard units and state and local police." Mayor Bartholomew F. Guida, having succeeded Lee, remembered the city riots of 1967 and noted, "The eyes of the nation will be on New Haven this weekend."

On Friday 12,000 to 15,000 youths, mostly white, protested on the Green and, despite a few isolated violent incidents, the demonstrations in support of the Black Panthers and against the Vietnam War were conducted peacefully *(see illustration on page 96)*. President Brewster, at the end, reaffirmed Yale's commitment to encourage and assist the efforts of the Law School faculty in observing the trial and to support further teaching and research in the proper treatment of minorities and radicals by the United States legal system. The Black Panther trials commenced in June and concluded the following year with the acquittal of Ericka Huggins and Bobby Seale, while George Sams was found guilty of giving the order, Lonnie McClucas of firing the first shot, and Warren Kimbro of firing the second shot that killed Rackley.

The accumulation of social and economic factors, including the riots of 1967 and later the Bobby Seale trial, worked against Lee's program of urban and human renewal. During his mayoral term, the population continued to decline and New Haven experienced further decay after he left office in 1969. According to a 1970 survey, "Goals for New Haven," there were seven main reasons for New Haven's continuing decline: (1) the city had lost 34,000 residents from 1950 to 1970 and these residents were disproportionately from the middle- and upper-income groups; (2) factories moved out of the city to other locations, creating higher unemployment while no new industries replaced them; (3) population and job movement out of the city created a lower tax base to pay for the social services of the increasingly poor population; (4) there were social unrest and racial tensions, heightened by state and federal welfare policies, that kept residents "locked in" poor neighborhoods; (5) crime and the fear of crime discouraged people from coming into the city and drew back the middle- and upper-income groups; (6) the decline in the quality of public school education encouraged families to move out of the city; and (7) houses were abandoned by the owners' inability to acquire loans and fire insurance.

Lee's program, nonetheless, was successful in certain areas. It rehabilitated over 9,000 dwelling units and replaced one-third of the city's old school buildings with new ones. He kept schools open for after-hour recreational activities and adult education. Wooster Square, which had deteriorated into a slum area, was transformed into a vibrant historical district, with many commercial and industrial buildings. It now boasts some of the best Italian restaurants in New Haven. Yale University, which supported Lee's urban renewal efforts, also added magnificent structures to its campus during the program, including Philip Johnson's Kline Biology Tower (1965), overlooking the city from Prospect Hill, and the Beinecke Rare Book and Manuscript Library (1963), a box structure designed by Gordon Bunshaft of Skidmore, Owings, and Merrill. It holds some of Yale's greatest treasures behind translucent marble walls. In a similar style, Marcel Breuer designed the Becton Engineering and Applied Center (1968) on Prospect Street.

Yale also hired Louis I. Kahn to design the Yale Art Gallery (1954), a four-story modern building with smooth walls of glass and brick. Eero Saarinen was hired to design the David S. Ingalls Hockey Rink (1958), known in the city as the "Yale Whale," as well as Morse College, Stiles College (1960), and the Yale Co-op Store (1961) with their earthy walls of poured granite. Paul Rudolph later built the Crawford Manor Housing for the Elderly (1965) on Park Street and designed the building for the Yale School of Art and Architecture (1963), a nine-story building with over 30 different levels. With Yale President Whitney Griswold's help, Lee transformed the city into an architectural marvel. "To his [Lee's] vast pride," the *New York Times* reported on August 27, 1967, "the city—long regarded nationally as no more than a vast unappealing slum one passed through to get to Yale—has become at least as much of an attraction to visitors as the university that dominated it for 200 years."

If Lee did not achieve all of his goals, there was no denying that he possessed a pioneering, bold, and imaginative spirit. He was a politician with vision and moral purpose, as he demonstrated in 1962 when his friend and political ally President John F. Kennedy came to New Haven to accept an honorary degree from Yale University. "You're missing all the fun in Washington, Dick," the President whispered in the ear of his friend. "You should have run for the Senate back in '58, when you had the chance." Lee, keeping his public appearance, replied to the President, "You and your damn hindsight advice. Where would you be if I hadn't stayed here and written your blueprint for the New Frontier?" Lee also received national recognition from President Johnson, who, after creating the Department of Housing and Urban Development in his War on Poverty, sent Lee one of the pens he used to sign the new housing act, saying, "You deserve a lion's share of the credit for efforts leading to the new department which will advance the progress of our cities." Lee, like George Dudley Seymour, believed that if you changed the physical environment, social benefits (like less poverty and crime) would naturally follow, but was he right? Did he fail? Who can tell? *(See illustration on page 97.)*

Other revitalization projects continued after Lee left office and some are still success stories for New Haven today. Architecturally, Marcel Breuer, who was responsible for the Becton Engineering and Applied Center (1968) and Pirelli Armstrong Rubber Company (1968), designed the East Rock Community School (1972) on Willow and Nash Streets. Robert Venturi and John Rauch designed the Dixwell Fire Station (1973). Douglas Orr, who had built the Community Services Building (1965) on State Street as well as the Yale Laboratory of Clinical Investigation (1965) on Davenport Avenue and the Yale Laboratory of Epidemiology and Public Health (1965) on College Street, designed the new Department of Police Services Headquarters (1973) on Union Avenue and the Air Rights Garage (1976–1980) on York Street. King Lui Wu, who had built the Manuscript Senior Society (1963), designed the Doctor's Office Building (1976) on Howard Avenue. Herbert S. Newman designed the Dixwell Community House (1970), State Plaza Office Building (1987), Whitney Grove Square (1987), and Audubon Court Housing and Stores (1988), and renovated the Union Railroad Station (1990) by adding a parking garage and City Hall (1994) by making additions while maintaining its Gothic Revival style. Robert Wendler also designed the Maritime Center and Garage (1988) on Long Wharf Drive and the Temple Medical Hotel (1991) on George Street. At the same time, Gerald M. Kagan built the Granite Square (1990) on State Street while Vincent C. Amore built the New Haven Foundation Building (1990) on Audubon Street.

Yale too added buildings during this period. It hired Louis I. Kahn again to design the Yale Center for British Art (1974), in a style often referred to as "brutalism" for its harsh, monolithic forms. The school also hired Frank O. Gehry to design the Yale Psychiatric Institute (1990) on Liberty Street, and Cesar Pelli, who had designed the One Century Tower (1990) on Church Street, to build the Yale Boyer Center for Molecular Medicine (1994) on Congress Avenue.

New Haven

Both private and public funds have contributed to the redevelopment of the city in the last two decades. During the 1980s, real estate entrepeneur Joel Shiavone, in a joint venture with First Constitution Bank, redeveloped Chapel Street between High and College Streets, transforming it into a small entertainment district with theaters, apartments, shops, and restaurants. Today he has begun to restore the historical—yet neglected—east side of the Quinnipiac River in the Fair Haven Heights neighborhood *(see illustration on page 98)*. The city, in the last decade, has also seen the completion of the Audubon Arts Center Complex (1994) while other revitalization projects are underway in Science Park, the East Shore community, the harbor front, and upper State Street.

Yale too has contributed to the redevelopment of the city. During the 1990s, with $4,000 in federal highway funds, it invested $2,000 in the Broadway District Project, tranforming Broadway Avenue into a small vibrant commercial district in the city. It also invested in the Ninth Square Project, an attempt to revitalize the neglected downtown square between Chapel, Church, George, and State Streets and restrucure the debt of the Chapel Square Mall. Although these last two projects have been less successful than the Broadway project, the university continues to support the city by investing in low-income housing projects and attracting high-tech companies to the area. As the largest employer in the region, accounting for over 11,000 direct jobs, it has contributed to the economic stability of the region and recently introduced the Yale Homebuyers Program, assisting employees in buying homes close to the city center. So far nearly 600 employees—of whom half are minorities and the majority are first-time homebuyers—have taken advantage of the program and received $25,000 each from the University. In the last decade, a cooperative working relationship has existed between the university and city. "I don't think you can point to a period in time," Mayor John DeStefano told the *Yale Daily News* on April 15, 2003, "in which the city and University have been as supportive of each other as has been the case over the last 10 years."

Since Lee's urban renewal program, many municipal improvements have been made across the city, but overall the economy has not performed well. According to the South Central Connecticut Regional Economic Development Corporation, or Regional Growth Partnership (RGP), which sponsored the writing of the Comprehensive Economic Development Strategy (CEDS) for the New Haven region in 2002, there are four main areas where the economy did not perform well:

> 1. During the 1990s, the regional economy grew at a slower rate than both the state and the nation. Total gross regional product (GRP) growth during the decade was slightly less than 20 percent in contrast to the state (33 percent) and the U.S. (38 percent). At the same time, the region's population increased by 1.9 percent, whereas the state grew at 3.6

percent and the country at 13 percent.

2. During the same period, the disparity of income between the rich and poor has increased. The poverty rates grew from 8.2 percent in 1990 to 9.7 percent in 2000, with one-half of the poor living in the city of New Haven itself.

3. Although Connecticut may be ranked as one of the wealthiest states in America, it has a number of poorly educated and low-income households in every major city, including New Haven and Meriden.

4. Between 1970 and 2000, more than 20,000 manufacturing jobs were lost and the share of all jobs for this category fell from 33 percent to about 15 percent of the entire workforce. Conversely, service sector jobs grew from 15 percent to about 35 percent. Despite this decline, however, manufacturing is still an important part of the region's economy, accounting for about 40,000 jobs today. By contrast, bioscience companies, which are more likely to drive future economic growth with a greater number of new jobs, employ slightly more than 10,000 workers.

In its survey, the CEDS has included the towns of Meriden, Hamden, Milford, West Haven, Wallingford, Branford, East Haven, North Haven, Guilford, Madison, North Branford, Orange, Woodbridge, Bethany, and the city of New Haven. In certain respects, this larger view has misrepresented the economic performance of the city, since New Haven during the 1980s and 1990s lagged behind the state in the creation of new jobs while, at the same time, the surrounding towns outperformed the state. In other words, suburban jobs have increased in the outer region by almost 30 percent since the 1980s, while in the city of New Haven there has been more than a 10 percent job loss, culminating in a 40 percentage-point job growth difference between the urban and suburban areas. To this day, and with the added loss of population decline and a lower tax base, as well as the added cost of protecting New Haven against a terrorist attack, the city has shown no signs of recovery and the unemployment rate, which typically has remained two to three percentage points higher than both the region and the state, was still one percent higher than the state average in the year 2000.

Consequently, New Haven has a higher rate of poverty than the rest of Connecticut. In 1980 it was, according to the federal census, the seventh-poorest city in the United States; in 2000, the poverty rate accounted for 24.4 percent of the population, having risen from 21.3 percent a decade earlier. The Connecticut average was 7.9, having risen from 6.8 percent. The following information is from the *Comprehensive Economic Development Strategy: South Central Connecticut Economic Development Corporation*:

Poverty Level in Connecticut and Greater New Haven

State and Towns	1990 Pop. below poverty level	2000 Pop. below poverty level
Connecticut	6.8%	7.9%
New Haven	21.3%	24.4%
Meriden	7.3%	11.0%
Hamden	4.4%	7.8%
Milford	3.7%	3.7%
West Haven	6.1%	8.8%
Wallingford	3.1%	3.6%
Branford	3.5%	4.1%
East Haven	4.9%	5.2%
North Haven	2.5%	3.5%
Guilford	3.0%	3.1%
Madison	1.5%	1.3%
North Branford	2.0%	1.6%
Orange	2.3%	2.5%
Woodbridge	2.1%	2.3%
Bethany	3.1%	2.6%

More alarmingly, the rate of poverty among children has risen to 32 percent, leaving one-third of New Haven's children in a state of poverty.

Children under the age of 18 living in poverty

Greater New Haven	1999 Children living in poverty
New Haven	32.0%
Meriden	17.0%
West Haven	12.0%
Hamden	9.0%
East Haven	5.0%
Wallingford	5.0%
Branford	4.5%
Milford	4.0%
Bethany	4.0%
Guilford	4.0%
Woodbridge	3.0%
North Haven	2.0%
Orange	2.0%
North Branford	1.0%
Madison	1.0%

As New Haven's population declined in the second half of the century, the city attracted larger concentrations of African Americans and Hispanics, indicating that race has a direct relationship with poverty. Between 1960 and 2000, for example, New Haven's white population (excluding Hispanics) dropped from about 128,000 to less than 44,000. At the same time, the black population increased from about 23,000 to over 46,000, and the Hispanic population from a little over 1,000 to over 26,000. The African-American community now comprises about 37 percent of the city's total popuation while the Hispanic community comprises over 20 percent. In addition, the federal census of 1990 determined that certain neighborhoods had a poverty rate as high as 40 to 50 percent, indicating neighborhoods like Newhallville, Dixwell, and the Hill, where there are large concentrations of African Americans, and Fair Haven, where there is a large concentration of Latinos. Peter Dobkin Hall's "Vital Signs: Organizational Population Trends and Civic Engagement in New Haven, Connecticut, 1850–1998" provides the following information:

New Haven Neighborhoods and African American Population (1996)

Neighborhood	% African American	Total Pop. of Neighborhood
High African-American Population		
Newhallville	94	7,798
Dixwell	85	6,298
Long Wharf	60	1,655
Dwight	50	6,799
Hill	50	17,420
Low African-American Population		
Central Business District	28	997
Yale	14	5,383
East Rock	7	9,290
Westville	10	6,904
Annex	8	5,362
Morris Cove	0.5	5,115

New Haven's earlier wealth, built largely on nineteenth-century industry, has all but disappeared in the last five to seven decades and the city, as it adjusts to the reality of a changing economy, has recently turned to its strengths, like higher education, healthcare, specialized areas of industry, and the arts, to improve its overall performance. As the largest employer in the region and one of the largest employers in the state of Connecticut, Yale University remains central to this economic recovery. Its world-class facilities, together with Yale-New Haven Hospital, biotech firms, medical device firms, and large pharmaceutical firms, has ensured the recent growth of the bioscience sector in the New Haven area. Jobs created in research and development have grown by an average 42 percent between the years 1995 and 1999, with as many as 10,000 jobs in the region.

Twenty-nine bioscience companies have emerged from research done at Yale and have attracted over $1.5 billion in private capital investment to the New Haven area, including the construction of a new building behind the School of Medicine by Pfizer. Many biotech companies are located on George Street or in Science Park and, besides creating new jobs, are an important tax base for the city. With companies like Bayer, Bristol-Myers Squibb, Boehringer

Ingleheim, and Pfizer, the biotech sector is working with the private sector, including Yale University, and finding new healthcare treatments.

Knowledge-based employment has been particularly strong in New Haven. As of 2002, about 19 percent of the region's jobs are in healthcare and private education; that is, about 29,000 jobs are in healthcare, namely Yale-New Haven Hospital, and about another 20,000 jobs are in the private educational sector, namely Yale University. Other knowledge-based employers in the region, though much smaller since the telecommunications and internet downturn during the late 1990s, include information technology, telecommunications, engineering, and consulting.

Despite the structural shift at the state and the national levels from a manufacturing to service-based economy, manufacturing is still an important component of the region's economy. About 40,000 jobs, or about 15 percent of the job base, are in the manufacturing sector and account for about 20 percent of the region's payroll. They are typically small firms (under 500 employees), requiring a highly skilled labor force, and are diverse, producing a wide variety of products like metals, chemicals, and pens. One area where there has been significant growth is the printing and publishing industry, which now employs over 3,000 workers. The *Comprehensive Economic Development Strategy: South Central Connecticut Economic Development Corporation* reported the following:

Manufacturing Sector 2000

	Employment	% of Manufactured Goods
Total Manufacturing	40,590	100 %
Apparel and Leather	720	1.8 %
Printing and Publishing	3,150	7.8 %
Chemical	3,270	8.1 %
Rubber and Miscellaneous Plastics	1,020	2.5 %
Primary Metals	1,670	4.1 %
Fabricated Metals	5,130	12.6 %
Machinery	3,510	8.6 %
Electrical and Trans. Equipment	7,780	19.2 %
Instruments	2,740	6.8 %
Other Manufacturing	11,580	28.5 %

Many of these new manufacturing jobs require highly-skilled laborers and, in some instances, overlap with jobs in the creative sector. Related to the knowledge-based sector, creative industries account for approximately 20,500 jobs in the region and include advertising, architecture, printing, film production and distribution, and media services. The New Haven architectural firm Cesar Pelli and Associates has established an international reputation while firms like Geometric Productions in New Haven, Guy Mark Studios in

Hamden, Headline Productions in Guilford, and Seven Seas Cinema Productions in Madison contribute to New Haven's growing creative sector.

With its close proximity to New York, one of New Haven's great strengths has been in the area of arts and entertainment. In the last two decades, African-American playwright August Wilson has premiered several of his plays at the Yale Repertory Theater, including his Pulitzer-Prize-winning *Fences* and *The Piano Lesson*. Founded in 1966 by Robert Brustein, dean of the Yale School of Drama (whose alumni include Julie Harris, Angela Bassett, Jane Kaczmarek, Frances McDormand, Chris Noth, John Turturro, Charles S. Dutton, Henry Hamlin, Ken Howard, Daniel J. Travanti, Liev Schreiber, Sigourney Weaver, Henry Winkler, Stacy Keach, Paul Newman, and Meryl Streep), the Repertory is a professional theater that has produced 90 world and American premieres, two of which have received Pulitzer Prizes. Ten of them have gone on to Broadway, earning nine Tony Awards, and the theater itself has received the Tony Award for Outstanding Regional Theater (1991), the Jujamcyn Theaters Award for "an outstanding contribution to the development and creative talent for the theater" (1992), and the Governor's Arts Award from Governor John Rowland for its (and the Yale School of Drama's) contribution to the arts in the state of Connecticut (2002).

Historically, New Haven has been one of the major theatrical centers in the United States. The Shubert, which is located in the city's theater district along College Street, has become one of the city's most notable performing arts centers for plays, dance, musicals, opera, and a variety of other musical performances. Since its founding in 1914 (closing temporarily during the 1970s), the Shubert has premiered over 600 Broadway plays, including *Robinson Crusoe, Jr., Oklahoma* (originally called *Away We Go*), *South Pacific*, *The King and I, The Sound of Music*, and *My Fair Lady*, as well as over 350 world and American premieres, including Tennessee Williams's *A Streetcar Named Desire* and Frank Wildhorn's *The Civil War*. Among the actors who received their first professional acclaim were Humphrey Bogart, Spencer Tracy, Katharine Hepburn, Jimmy Stewart, Clark Gable, Mary Martin, Gene Kelly, Marlon Brando, Robert Redford, Warren Beatty, Shirley MacLaine, Andy Griffith, Jane Fonda, Sidney Poitier, James Garner, Dyan Cannon, James Earl Jones, Liza Minnelli, Ken Howard, Robert Guillaume, and John Travolta.

Another important theater in the city of New Haven is the Long Wharf Theater. Founded in 1965 by two Yale students, it has two fully-equipped stages and has sent over 20 productions to Broadway or Off-Broadway, including Pulitzer-Prize-winning *Wit* and *The Gin Game*, as well as *Travels with My Aunt, All My Sons, Down the Garden Paths, Red, Mystery School, Hughie, Broken Glass, American Buffalo, Requiem for a Heavyweight, Ah, Wilderness!*, and *Quartermaine's Terms*. It has also premiered a number of notable plays, including Arthur Miller's *The Crucible* and Michael Christofer's Pulitzer-Prize winning *The Shadow Box*, and its productions of *The Changing Room, The Contractor,* and

New Haven

Streamers each received the New York Drama Critics Circle Award for Best Play. Moreover, the Yale Rep has received many Tony Awards and nominations, including the 1978 Tony Award for Outstanding Regional Theater, Obie Awards for Ensemble Performance, and the Margo Jones Award for "production of new works." During its short history, Long Wharf has become an internationally-renowned theater, drawing regular audience members from as far afield as New York and Boston. Together with the Yale Rep and Shubert, it is still one of New Haven's cultural and economic strengths and has more to offer, as do New Haven's other theaters, which include the Palace on College Street, the University Theater on York Street, and the Little Theater located in the Educational Center for the Arts on Audubon Street.

In addition to the theater, New Haven has cultivated a strong arts and entertainment community. Since 1996, for example, the city has hosted the International Festival of Arts and Ideas, a two-week-long festival celebrating artists and thinkers from around the world. In it opening year, it drew 60,000 visitors from the the Greater New Haven area, as well as visitors from other countries. Having grown since then, it now attracts almost 200,000 visitors annually. Other arts and entertainment events in the city include the Summer Jazz Festival, City Wide Open (Arts) Studios, Film Festival, Ice Sculpture Exhibit and Competition, and Concerts in the Parks, not to mention the contributions of the New Haven Symphony Orchestra (established in 1894), New Haven Chorale, Connecticut Gay Men's Chorus, Chancel Opera Company, and the New Haven Ballet.

Another cultural and economic strength in the New Haven area are its museums. The Eli Whitney Museum, established in 1979, is located on the Mill River site where Whitney built his musket factory in 1798. It offers an assortment of workshops, exhibits, programs, lectures, and entertainment for both adults and children. The Shoreline Trolley Museum on River Street in East Haven houses over 100 trolleys from 1904–1939 and has a three-mile trolley ride for children through the shoreline woods and wetlands. The 102nd Infantry Regiment Museum and National Guard Armory on Goffe Street houses hundreds of rare artifacts from the Civil War period to the present, displaying New Haven's military past, and has its own library. The New Haven Colony Historical Society, established in 1862, offers the best collection of New Haven artifacts and manuscripts. Located on Whitney Avenue in a Georgian Colonial-Revival building, the society has both a library and a museum that is open to the public, in addition to the Pardee-Morris House, a late colonial home on Lighthouse Road that is open to the public seasonally.

Other historical societies and museums in the Greater New Haven area include the Jewish Historical Society on Davenport Avenue; the Ukrainian Heritage Center on George Street; the Knights of Columbus Museum and Archives on State Street; the Irish American Historical Society in East Haven;

the Huntington Historical Society in Shelton; the Trumbull Historical Society and the Woods Estate, both in Trumbull; the Milford Wharf Lane Complex in Milford; the Osborne Homestead Museum in Derby; the Allis-Bushel House and Museum in Madison; the Lock 12 Historic Park and Museum in Cheshire; the Jonathan Dickerman House in Hamden; the Thomas Darling House in Woodbridge; the Stone-Otis House in Orange; the Hotchkiss Farmhouse in Prospect; and the Hyland House, Thomas Griswold House, and the Henry Whitefield House Museum in Guilford.

As one of the main supporters of cultural life in New Haven, Yale University has also built a number of world-class museums and art galleries that are now open to the public. In 1866, for example, it founded the Peabody Museum, which is one of the largest and oldest museums of natural history in the country, housing a large assortment of dinosaur fossils and human and natural curiosities. Earlier, in 1832, Yale founded the first university art gallery in North America after John Trumbull donated over 100 of his paintings to the college. Today the Yale University Art Gallery is one of the most prestigious university art galleries in the world, housing over 100,000 paintings and objects. Complementing the gallery is the Yale Center for British Art, established in 1966 after Paul Mellon, a Yale graduate, donated his collection of British art to his *alma mater*. Today the center houses over 50,000 paintings, prints, drawings, watercolors, and rare books, the most comprehensive collection outside of Great Britain. In addition to the Beinecke Library, which houses more than 500,000 rare books and millions of manuscripts, the university has also established the Yale Collection of Musical Instruments, containing over 850 European and American instruments from the sixteenth to the twenty-first centuries.

New Haven's cultural strengths, including Yale University itself, attract a number of visitors to the region each year. In the future they will contribute to the city's economic recovery and growth, but before this can happen, the city needs to rejuvenate its dying retail sector. The exodus of middle- to upper-middle income groups from the city center and the shift of the retail sector to the suburbs over the last 50 years have devastated this sector. City officials are still attempting to rejuvenate the downtown retail sector and are beginning to turn their attention to the harbor front, a potentially vibrant retail and tourist location for the twenty-first century. Although plans for the Long Wharf Mall Galleria came to a sudden end at the turn of the millennium when an Australian-based company, Westfield, blocked the city's plans for a mega-mall project, there are still plans underway for a new hotel as well as the opening of an Ikea outlet by the end of 2004. Predominantly known for its industry, New Haveners have not yet taken full advantage of their natural harbor, creating a nucleus of commercial and tourist activity while preserving the natural environment along the coast *(see illustration on page 98)*. With $1 billion in public and institutional construction projects underway or planned in the New

Haven region over the next five years, city officials will need to focus their energies on redeveloping Long Wharf, transforming it into a vibrant commercial and cultural center while preserving the natural landscape.

For the last decade, Mayor John DeStefano Jr. has pursued the renewal initiative, what some have called "The Livable City Initiative," focusing his attention on housing and neighborhood revitalization, the return of an AHL hockey team to the Coliseum, and the redevelopment of the downtown New Haven area. He explained in "Strategies for Financial Recovery: The City of New Haven Experience," an article in the *Government Finance Review* 15 (June 1999), when the current administration came to office in 1994:

> the city had little money in the bank and its credit was so shaky that it could hardly borrow. The city's population had fallen to about 125,000, while it lost 18 percent of its manufacturing jobs in only three years. To make matters worse, the city's public buildings and infrastructure were crumbling, while its fiscal health continued to deteriorate and its shrinking tax base smothered plans for capital investment. Looming just behind the budget deficit was a cash shortfall that delayed vendor payments. Meanwhile city officials were wasting precious general fund dollars to subsidize the operation of assets once intended to be self-supporting.

And five years later:

> New Haven is a reborn American city. City Officials have returned the jurisdiction back to a sound fiscal footing and are recreating a place where children learn in good schools, residents live in safe neighborhoods, and everyone has the opportunity to make the most of his or her talents. The city has accomplished this by following a path that avoids temporary, quick fixes in favor of creating a climate for sustainable economic growth and social well-being. New Haven has regenerated itself through competition and compassion.

DeStefano's renewal initiative has brought improvements to parts of the city, but as Peter Dobkin Hall of the Harvard John F. Kennedy School of Government pointed out at a conference on "Property Tax Exemption for Charities" in Washington, D.C., to be published in Evelyn Brody's and Elizabeth Boris's forthcoming *Property Tax Exemptions and Nonprofit Organizations*:

> In fact, few residents of New Haven would recognize the Mayor's effusive description as being one of their hometown. While he had succeeded in achieving fiscal soundness and safe neighborhoods (thanks to a pioneering community policing program), the schools remained among the lowest scoring in Connecticut on statewide mastery tests, two-thirds of the city's school-age children still lived below the poverty line, and the city continued to lose tax-paying businesses (including the largest private taxpayer, the Southern New England Telephone Company). Efforts to promote "sustainable economic growth" proved disappointing as businesses lured to the

city with generous tax breaks failed to fulfill their commitments to the city. Resources were diverted into enterprises that employed few residents and contributed nothing to the tax base, like an annual corporation-sponsored tennis tournament, a minor league baseball team, and an International Festival of Arts and Ideas. Little went into creating and maintaining the kind of communications, information, and transportation infrastructure needed to attract new businesses. New Haven went through most of the decade of the 1990s without an operating quality hotel. Its airport, refurbished early in the mid-1990s to handle the crowds who attended the International Special Olympics, was abandoned by major airlines because of inadequate facilities. New Haven—and Connecticut generally—lagged far behind comparable cities in making high-speed broad-band internet access available (DSL lines only began to be installed in the winter of 2000).

As for Yale University's tax exempt status as a billion-dollar property owner, a recurring complaint among some residents, the fact remains that the university is the city's second-largest taxpayer, behind United Illuminating, the largest real-estate taxpayer, and the city's largest producer of revenue. The city receives close to $19 million (about 77¢ on the dollar) from the state's PILOT program ("payments in lieu of taxes") for Yale's tax-exempt properties and close to $2 million from the university for its commercial properties, plus another $2 million in voluntary funds for fire department protection and other services. In other words, Yale is an important contributor not only to the city and its future but also to the region as a whole. It employs over 11,000 individuals in the region, has committed over $100 million to the community in the last decade, and is now involved in promoting business opportunities in the city. But as Hall has further remarked, "In connection with the Mayor's statements about getting Yale involved with small business development in the community," he has "pointed to the university's investments in the Broadway area of retail shops and the Ninth Square retail-residential development (an ambitious effort to bring middle class residents back to the Central Business District)." What he has not mentioned, however, "was that the Broadway redevelopment had displaced a dozen small locally-owned businesses and replaced them with national chain outlets, including Barnes & Noble (which displaced the Yale Co-op) and Trailblazer." And so renewal is an ongoing process; there is more work to be done, and the emergence of terrorist threats to America's homeland makes the job that much more difficult for the mayor and city officials.

EPILOGUE

Between 8:45 and 9:03 a.m. on September 11, 2001, United and American Airlines flights 11 and 175 flew into the North and South towers of the World Trade Center in New York. Shortly afterwards, American Airlines Flight 77 flew into the west side of the Pentagon and United Airlines Flight 93 crashed in Shanksville, Pennsylvania. America awoke to the tragedies, shocked, angry, and saddened. Had a foreign power attacked the homefront? Were they acts of terrorism, foreign or national? These were questions on the minds of many Americans as the events of September 11 unfolded. The media and government quickly responded by identifying the events as acts of terrorism and by connecting them with Al Qaeda, an international terrorist organization with training camps in Afghanistan. At first the leadership of Al Qaeda, many of whom were living in Afghanistan under the protection of the Taliban regime, were aloof and denied any responsibility, but when President George Bush adopted a U.S. foreign policy of "preemption" and an American invasion of Afghanistan became imminent, the Al Qaeda leadership confessed to its role and indeed seemed to revel in it.

The U.S. foreign policy of preemption was one way in which the government responded to the events of September 11. Another was homeland security, protecting the nation against further threats of terrorism. In October 2001, President Bush created the Department of Homeland Security, appointing Tom Ridge its first director. State and local governments also took a role in defending the homefront. Towns and cities across the nation reorganized their infrastructure and budgets to deal with the new threat of international terrorism. In New Haven, where urban rejuvenation had been an ongoing process since the mid-twentieth century, the cost of security cut into the city's budget and diverted attention from other municipal initiatives.

In the aftermath of September 11, President Bush proposed a federal package of $3.5 billion to state and local governments. The money, intended to bolster local and state security, was not forthcoming, however. New Haven, like other cities and states, was forced to swallow the cost itself. Without federal funds, the city bought equipment and trained members of its fire department for a chemical or biological attack; it did its best to protect key strategic points of the city, including bridges, the harbor, the Pitkin Tunnel, and the Tweed-New Haven Airport. A year later, the city still had no federal funding as it prepared for an "Emergency Preparedness Tabletop Exercise" at City Hall, a test scenario of how city officials would respond to a bioterrorist attack.

Epilogue

"Terrorists have clearly identified that it is cities they will attack," said Mayor DeStefano to a reporter for *The Yale Herald* on September 6, 2002, "places where people live together, where the icons of our society and our communities exist. Cities have a responsibility to be prepared to respond to those attacks and to protect against those attacks. . . . The Federal government has not been a partner in this. We have to take on our own defense responsibilities."

Five months later, according to the *New York Times* (February 13, 2003), the city still had no federal funding and the situation had improved little, if at all, since the tragedy. "The bottom line for us," exclaimed New Haven's mayor, "is that we are no better off than we were on Sept. 11, that we're not ready for a terrorist strike."

This was no understatement. By April, the city had outfitted no more than 10 percent of its 300 firefighters with the proper protective equipment for responding to a chemical or biological attack. And by late November, Mayor DeStefano, in a speech before the National Press Club, spoke of the need for more federal funding for the security of America's cities:

> In the two years since the 9-11 attacks, this nation has yet to strike a balance between homeland security and day-to-day public safety. At a time when the nation's police forces are expected to be on guard against terrorism and to serve as "first responders" in the event of a terrorist incident, Washington is actually cutting funding for basic public safety programs.

Without ensuring security, the mayor added, "we cannot create the economic growth or quality of life" so essential to the preservation and growth of the urban middle class.

Three weeks after DeStefano's speech, U.S. Senators Chris Dodd and Joe Lieberman announced that the Department of Homeland Security was awarding close to $4 million in port security grants to the state of Connecticut. Bridgeport, with the largest port, received the lion's share of $3,191,090, followed by New Haven with $561,089, New London with $50,000, and Stamford with $23,386. More recently, the Department of Homeland Security approved $9.5 million for the city and surrounding towns, meaning that New Haven will soon receive more Homeland Security funding per capita than any other city in the United States. The port and Buckeye Pipeline, as well as the presence of Yale University and the city's geographical location in a highly dense area between New York and Boston, as city officials have pointed out, make the city an attractive target for a future terrorist attack.

Despite this new source of revenue, the city is still paying for its security. The federal package, which will be used to strengthen high-risk areas of the city, purchase rescue equipment, upgrade communications equipment, and train first responders, cannot be used to pay for the salaries of policemen, firefighters, or emergency medical technicians. The city will, therefore, have to cover these costs. At the same time, it has to address recent state budget cuts that have cut municipal aid to the cities and led to tax increases and municipal cuts in areas like education. More recently, the federal government has passed a budget resolution through Congress that will cut $213 million in federal money over the next ten years for the state of Connecticut, portending further cuts or tax increases at both the state and local levels.

Today New Haven officials are facing new challenges as state and federal budget cuts and the cost of defending the homefront divert both time and money from earlier municipal initiatives, but the answer might not lie with more government spending. As Douglas Rae, Yale Professor of Management and Political Science, revealed in *City: Urbanism and Its End* (2003), government spending has repeatedly failed to restore urban vitality in New Haven. Instead, he has put forward the model of the early "urbanist" decades of the twentieth century, when New Haven's neighborhoods were a mixture of houses, apartments, saloons, restaurants, barbers, delis, and small grocery stores, and has argued for a variant, modern form of mixed-use city life. The city's future, in other words, has less to do with government initiatives than with unplanned civic engagements, mixed-use neighborhoods, and a large enough middle class to support urban neighborhoods. "Government in general," he concluded after working as a chief administrating official in City Hall, "can accomplish a lot less than people realize."

Indeed, during the second half of the twentieth century, City Hall failed in certain areas, namely in reversing the trend of outward migration of business and middle-class groups to the suburbs, but it also succeeded in other areas, namely in historic revitalization, public housing, and community policing. Since 1996, for example, the city has rehabilitated over 500 housing units, trained over 500 residents in homeownership, and enforced stronger housing-code regulations. Moreover, it has improved public housing by replacing crowded housing projects with single-family homes. Typically these new homes, like the Monterey Homes that replaced the Elm Haven projects in the Dixwell neighborhood, have lawns and encourage a sense of civic pride among residents and families living in them.

To what degree local government has a role to play in the restoration of urban vitality is very much a question of political affiliation or persuasion, but most people believe the promotion and preservation of local culture and traditions are the responsibility of government. In New Haven, for example, the St. Patrick's Day Parade—first sponsored by the New Haven Hibernian Provident Society on March 17, 1842, and later with the help of the Associated Irish Societies—has become the largest non-commercial parade in New England. It is also the oldest St. Patrick's Day Parade in New England and the sixth oldest in the country. As a voluntary event, the city does not sponsor or organize the parade, but it does provide police protection and services, and participates in the event with its marching bands from the schools, police department, and fire departments.

Epilogue

Another New Haven event, one that has evoked civic pride since the beginning of the twentieth century, is "Powder-House Day." In *Three Centuries of New Haven*, Rollin Osterweis recalled the annual celebration as one of the exciting features of springtime:

> Many a 20th-century citizen has preserved as the most vivid recollection of his childhood the picture of men in tall bearskin hats, red coats, white knee breeches, and black leggings, marching and countermarching across the lower Green. Then comes the exciting climax: the Foot Guards draw up in formation in front of the City Hall and their officers march over to the steps, where the mayor awaits them; the carefully rehearsed dialogue follows; "Captain Benedict Arnold," "Lieutenant Jesse Leavenworth," and the rest return to their troops triumphantly carrying a set of keys. Excited children beg their parents for explanations of the drama, and learn the story of "the demand for the keys to the Powder-House."

More recently the city, with the assistance of individual and business sponsorships, has launched a new tradition, hosting the International Festival of Arts and Ideas. Today the summer festival attracts close to 200,000 visitors each year, bringing both cultural and economic benefits to the city and the south-central region of Connecticut.

Such success stories illustrate the important role of government in promoting and preserving cultural life and traditions in the city. They are an integral part of urban life, bringing residents and visitors together in an urban setting. And yet New Haven has lost some of these traditions. For example, during the winter months of the second half of the nineteenth and for part of the twentieth century, one often saw children and families ice skating or playing ice hockey on the lower end of the Green *(see illustration on page 99)*. The New Haven Fire Department had begun the custom of flooding the southeast corner of the Green in the early 1860s, but at some point in the twentieth century the custom came to an end.

Another loss for city of New Haven was the removal of the Franklin Elm in 1904 *(see illustration on page 100)*. According to tradition, Jerry Allen, a "poet and pedagogue," carried the tree on his back from Hamden Plains and sold it to Thaddeus Beecher for a pint of beer and some trifles. On April 17, 1790, the same day Benjamin Franklin died in Philadelphia, it was planted on the southeast corner of the Green and grew to a height of 80 feet before its removal at the beginning of the twentieth century. Elm disease had damaged the tree, leading to its removal, but no one thought to mark the spot with a memorial or plaque.

Although these traditions might seem small or insignificant on the surface, they are an important part of our cultural memory. As New Haveners look to their future, to what will be, they are—though unknowingly at times—looking to their past as well, to individuals like James Hillhouse, Donald Grant

Mitchell, and George Dudley Seymour, who helped to make New Haven a "City Beautiful." They are listening to the words of Colonel Isaac L. Ullman, who, as president of the New Haven Chamber of Commerce, said on March 31, 1909:

> In our efforts to secure new enterprises, we have, I believe, been pursuing the wrong policy and have been working from the wrong standpoint. While we should continue unabated our efforts to secure new industrial enterprises to locate in New Haven, and should seek to have people come here to reside, we should, in order to more easily accomplish this, endeavor to make the city of New Haven so attractive, both as a residential and as a manufacturing center, that its very attractiveness will invite the manufacturer and the citizen of other communities to come among us and become a part of our industrial and social life.
>
> This attractiveness can be secured if we see to it that this city has a most excellent school system; that it has well-paved and well-lighted streets; that it has a capable and efficient health board, with the necessary powers and facilities to enable such a board to protect and conserve the health of our citizens; that our beautiful trees are preserved, so that our city may continue to be known in the future, as it has ever been in the past, as the "City of Elms;" and withal, a rate of taxation as low as is consistent with the needs of a live and progressive community. In short, we should try to make it, as nearly as we can, a "City Beautiful" in fact."

Ullman spoke these words in an age of civic voluntarism, when citizens were more willing to contribute and partake in city life and the beautification of their city. And so we are reminded of our responsibility as private citizens and business leaders—that we too have a role to play in restoring urban vitality, not just the government.

BIBLIOGRAPHY

PRIMARY AND SECONDARY TEXTS

Andrews, Charles M. *The Rise and Fall of the New Haven Colony*. New Haven: Published for the Tercentenary Commission by the Yale University Press, 1936.

Atwater, Edward Elias, ed. *History of the City of New Haven to the Present Time*. 2 vols. New York: W.W. Munsell & Co., 1887.

Barber, John W. *History and Antiquities of New Haven (Conn.): From Its Earliest Settlement to the Present Time*. New Haven: J.W. Barber, 1831–1832.

Brown, Elizabeth Mills. *New Haven: A Guide to Architecture and Urban Design*. New Haven and London: Yale University Press, 1976.

Butler, Jon. *Awash in a Sea of Faith: Christianizing the American People*. Cambridge, MA: Harvard University Press, 1990.

Calder, Isabel MacBeath. *The New Haven Colony*. New Haven: Yale University Press, 1934; reprinted Hamden, CT: Archon Books, 1970.

De Forest, John W. *History of the Indians of Connecticut: From the Earliest Known Period to 1850*. Hamden, CT: Archon Books, 1964.

Dexter, Franklin Bowditch. *Sketch of the History of Yale University*. New York: H. Holt and Company, 1887.

———, ed. *Ancient Town Records: New Haven Town Records, 1649–1684*. 2 vols. New Haven: New Haven Colony Historical Society, 1917–1919.

Hegel, Richard. *Nineteenth-Century Historians of New Haven*. Hamden, CT: Archon Books, 1972.

Mitchell, Mary H. *History of New Haven County, Connecticut*. Chicago and Boston: The Pioneer Historical Publishing Co., 1930.

Hoadly, Charles J., ed. *Records of the Colony and Plantation of New Haven, 1638–1649*. Hartford: Tiffany and Company, 1857.

Howe, Irving, and Kenneth Libo. *How We Lived, A Documentary History of Immigrant Jews in America, 1880–1930*. New York: Richard Marek Publishers, 1979.

Jones, Howard. *Mutiny on the Amistad: The Saga of a Slave Revolt and Its Impact on American Abolition, Law, and Diplomacy*. New York: Oxford University Press, 1987.

Lambert, Ruth. *Harrison's Illustrated Guide: Greater New Haven*. New Haven: Real Estate Educational Foundation, Inc., 1995.

League of Women Voters of New Haven. *New Haven: A Handbook on City*

Government and Services. New Haven: League of Women Voters of New Haven, Inc., 1971.

Levermore, Charles H. *Town and City Government of New Haven.* Baltimore: N. Murray, Johns Hopkins University Press, 1886.

Kitz, Christopher. *Democracy in New Haven: A History of the Board of Aldermen, 1638–1988.* New Haven: The Board of Aldermen of the City of New Haven, 1988.

Lossing, Benjamin J. *The Pictorial Field-Book of the Revolution; or, Illustrations, by Pen and Pencil, of the History, Biography, Scenery, Relics, and Traditions of the War for Independence.* 2 vols., New York: Harper & Brothers, 1851–1852.

———. *Lives of Celebrated Americans: Comprising Biographies of Three Hundred and Forty Eminent Persons.* Hartford: Thomas Belknap, 1869.

———. *Our Country: A Household History for All Readers, from the Discovery of America to the One Hundredth Anniversary of the Declaration of Independence.* 3 vols., New York: Johnson, Wilson & Co., 1875–1878.

Mininberg, Mark J. *Saving New Haven: John W. Murphy Meets the Crisis of the Great Depression.* New Haven: Fine Arts Publications, 1988.

New Haven Colony Historical Society, *The* Amistad *Story.* New Haven: New Haven Colony Historical Society, 2000.

Osterweis, Rollin Gustav. *Three Centuries of New Haven, 1638–1938.* New Haven: Yale University Press, 1953.

Philie, William L. *Change and Tradition: New Haven, Connecticut, 1780–1830.* New York and London: Garland Publishing, Inc., 1990.

Powers, Zara Jones, ed. *Ancient Town Records: New Haven Town Records, 1684–1769.* New Haven: New Haven Colony Historical Society, 1962.

Rae, Douglas W. *City: Urbanism and Its End.* New Haven: Yale University Press, 2003.

Shumway, Floyd, and Richard Hegel, eds. *New Haven: An Illustrated History.* Woodland Hills, CA: Windsor Publications, 1987.

Stewart, Daniel Y. *Black New Haven, 1920–1977.* New Haven: Advocate Press, Inc., 1977.

Talbot, Allan R. *The Mayor's Game: Richard Lee of New Haven and the Politics of Change.* New York: Harper and Row, 1967.

Warner, Robert Austin. *New Haven Negroes: A Social History.* New Haven: Yale University Press, 1940.

White, David O. *Connecticut's Black Soldiers, 1775–1783.* Chester, CT: Pequot Press, 1973.

Williams, Yohuru. *Black Politics/White Power: Civil Rights, Black Power, and the Black Panthers in New Haven.* New York: Brandywine Press, 2000.

Zeichner, Oscar. *Connecticut's Years of Controversy, 1750–1776.* Chapel Hill: University of North Carolina Press, 1949.

Bibliography

ARTICLES AND CHAPTERS

Archer, John. "Puritan Town Planning in New Haven." *Journal of the Society of Architectural Historians*, XXXIV (1975), p. 140–149.

Bacon, Leonard. "Civil Government in New Haven Colony." *Papers of the New Haven Colony Historical Society,* I (1865), p. 11–28.

Baldwin, Ernest H. "Why New Haven Is Not a State of the Union." *Papers of the New Haven Colony Historical Society,* VII (1908), 161–187.

Baldwin, Simeon E. "The Captives of the *Amistad*." *Papers of the New Haven Colony Historical Society*, IV (1888), p. 331–370.

———. "The Three Constitutions of Connecticut," *Papers of the New Haven Colony Historical Society,* V (1894), p. 179–246.

Bickford, Christopher P. "Connecticut and Its Charter." *Connecticut Historical Society Bulletin*, IXL (1984), p. 110–123.

Bremer, Francis J. "The New Haven Colony and Oliver Cromwell." *Connecticut Historical Society Bulletin*, XXXVIII (July 1973), p. 65–72.

DeStefano, John Jr. "Strategies for Financial Recovery: The City of New Haven Experience." *Government Finance Review* XV (June 1999), p. 21–3.

Dexter, Franklin Bowditch. "New Haven in 1784." *Papers of the New Haven Colony Historical Society*, IV (1888), p. 117–138.

———. "Notes on Some of the New Haven Loyalists, Including Those Graduated at Yale." *Papers of the New Haven Colony Historical Society,* IX (1918), p. 29–45.

Farnham, Thomas J. "New Haven, 1638–1690." in Floyd Shumway and Richard Hegel, eds., *New Haven: An Illustrated History* (Woodland Hills, CA: Windsor Publications, 1987), p. 9–24.

Fowler, David H. "Connecticut's Freemen: The First Forty Years." *William and Mary Quarterly*, 3rd Ser., XV (1958), p. 312–333.

Fowler, William C. "The Historical Status of the Negro, in Connecticut." *The Historical Magazine*, 3rd Ser., III (1874), p. 12–18.

Goodrich, Chauncey. "Invasion of New Haven by the British Troops, July 5, 1779," *Papers of the New Haven Colony Historical Society,* II (1877), p. 31–92.

Hall, Peter Dobkin. "Vital Signs: Organizational Population Trends and Civic Engagement in New Haven, Connecticut, 1850–1998." In Theda Skocpol and Morris P. Fiorina, eds., *Civic Engagement in American Democracy.* (Washington, D.C.: Brookings Institution Press, 1999), p. 211–248.

———. "Is Tax Exemption Intrinsic or Contingent? The Tax Treatment of Voluntary Associations, Non-Profit Organizations, and Religious Bodies in New Haven, Connecticut, 1750–2000." In Evelyn Brody and Elizabeth Boris, eds*., Property Tax Exemptions and Nonprofit Organizations* (Washington, D.C.: Urban Institute, forthcoming).

Hart, Samuel. "The Fundamental Orders and the Charter." *Papers of the New Haven Colony Historical Society*, VIII (1914), p. 238–254.

Kennedy, Ruby Jo Reeves. "Single or Triple Melting Pot? Intermarriage

Trends in New Haven, 1870–1940." *American Journal of Sociology*, XLIX (1944), p. 331–339.

Kuslan, Louis I. "New Haven Industry: A Retrospective View." In Floyd Shumway and Richard Hegel, eds., *New Haven: An Illustrated History* (Woodland Hills, CA: Windsor Publications, 1987), p. 77–93.

Leonard, Ira M. "The Rise of Metropolitan New Haven, 1860 to 1980." In Floyd Shumway and Richard Hegel, eds., *New Haven: An Illustrated History* (Woodland Hills, CA: Windsor Publications, 1987), p. 45–61.

Lines, Edwin S. "Jared Ingersoll, Stamp Master, and the Stamp Act." *Papers of the New Haven Colony Historical Society,* IX (1918), p. 174–200.

Lipson, Dorothy Ann. "From Puritan Village to Yankee City, 1690 to 1860." In Floyd Shumway and Richard Hegel, eds., *New Haven: An Illustrated History* (Woodland Hills, CA: Windsor Publications, 1987), p. 29–43.

Leonard, Ira M. "The Rise of Metropolitan New Haven, 1860 to 1980," in Floyd Shumway and Richard Hegel, eds., *New Haven: An Illustrated History* (Woodland Hills, CA: Windsor Publications, 1987), p. 45–61.

Menschel, David. "Abolition Without Deliverence: The Law of Connecticut Slavery 1784–1848." *Yale Law Journal*, CXI (2001), p. 183–222.

Mitchell, Mary H. "Slavery in Connecticut and Especially in New Haven." *Papers of the New Haven Colony Historical Society,* X (1951), p. 286–312.

Morgan, Edmund S. "Ezra Stiles: The Education of a Yale Man, 1742–1746." *Huntington Library Quarterly*, XVII (1954), p. 251–268.

Norton, Frederick Calvin. "Negro Slavery in Connecticut." *Connecticut Magazine*, V (1899), p. 320–328.

Parker, Edwin P. "The Congregationlist Separates of the Eighteenth Century in Connecticut." *Papers of the New Haven Colony Historical Society*, VIII (1914), p. 151–161.

Pearson, Ralph L. and Linda Wrigley. "Before Mayor Richard Lee: George Dudley Seymour and City Planning Movement in New Haven, 1907–1924." *Journal of Urban History*, VI (1980), p. 297–319.

Richards, David Alan. "New Haven and Stamp Act Crisis of 1765–1766." *Yale University Library Gazette*. VIL (1971), p. 67–85.

———. "New Haven's Charter Quest and Annexation by Connecticut." *Connecticut History*, XXIX (1988), p. 16–26.

Schiff, Judith A. "The Social History of New Haven." In Floyd Shumway and Richard Hegel, eds., *New Haven: An Illustrated History* (Woodland Hills, CA: Windsor Publications, 1987), p. 95–113.

Schofield, Mary-Pearl. "The Three Judges of New Haven." *History Today*, XII (1962), p. 346–353.

Steiner, Bernard C., "Governor William Leete and the Absorption of New Haven Colony by Connecticut," in *Annual Report of the American Historical Association* (Washington: G.P.O., 1892), p. 209–222.

Stone, B. Charles. "The Invasion of New Haven: July 1779." *Connecticut Heritage*

Magazine (July 1989), p. 16–20.

Townshend, Charles. "The Quinnipiac Indians." *Papers of the New Haven Colony Historical Society,* VI (1900), p. 151–219.

Welles, Lemuel A. "The Loss of the Charter Government in Connecticut." *Papers of the New Haven Colony Historical Society,* IX (1918), p. 90–128.

Wiedersheim, William A. "New Haven Architecture." In Floyd Shumway and Richard Hegel, eds., *New Haven: An Illustrated History* (Woodland Hills, CA: Windsor Publications, 1987), p. 131–152.

White, Henry. "The New Haven Colony." *Papers of the New Haven Colony Historical Society,* I (1865), p. 1–10.

————. "New Haven's Adventure on the Delaware Bay." *Papers of the New Haven Colony Historical Society,* IV (1888), p. 209–230.

DOCTORIAL DISSERTATIONS AND OTHER THESES

Luchowski, Linda Susan. "Sunshine Soldiers: New Haven and the American Revolution." Doctoral Dissertation, State University of New York, 1976.

Jerome K. Myers. "The Differential Time Factor in Assimilation: A Study of Aspects and Processes of Assimilation among the Italians of New Haven." Doctoral Dissertation, Yale University, 1950.

Johnston, William Michael. "On the Outside Looking In: Irish, Italian and Black Ethnic Politics in an American City." Doctoral Dissertation, Yale University, 1977.

Miller, Morty. "New Haven: The Italian Community." History Essay, Yale University, 1969.

Philie, William Lewis. "Change and Tradition: New Haven, Connecticut, 1780–1830." Doctoral Dissertation, University of Maine, 1984.

Rindler, Edward Paul. "The Migration from the New Haven Colony to Newark, East New Jersey: A Study of Puritan Values and Behavior, 1630–1720." Doctoral Dissertation, University of Pennsylvania, 1977.

Roetger, Robert West. "Order and Disorder in Early Connecticut: New Haven, 1639–1701." Doctoral Dissertation, University of New Hampshire, 1982.

Shumway, Floyd Mallory. "Early New Haven and Its Leadership." Doctoral Dissertation, Columbia University, 1968.

Sorenson, Charles William. "Response to Crisis: An Analysis of New Haven, 1638–1665." Doctoral Dissertation, Michigan State University, 1973.

VanBeek, Elizabeth Tucker. "Piety and Profit: English Puritans and the Shaping of a Godly Marketplace in the New Haven Colony." Doctoral Dissertation, University of Virginia, 1993.

INDEX

Index